YURTS

YURTS
living in the round

BECKY KEMERY

Gibbs Smith, Publisher
Salt Lake City

This book is dedicated to my parents, B. Peter Kemery and Evelyn Thomas Kemery, world travelers and hosts extraordinaire—in thanks for instilling a love of learning and a fascination with other cultures, and for your ongoing support of this project.

First Edition
10 09 08 07   5 4 3 2

Text © 2006 Becky Kemery
Photographs © 2006 as noted on page 144

PUBLISHED BY
Gibbs Smith, Publisher
PO Box 667
Layton, Utah 84041

Orders: 1 [800] 835-4993
www.gibbs-smith.com

Designed by Steve Rachwal
Printed and bound in Hong Kong

Library of Congress Cataloging-in-Publication Data
Kemery, Becky.
    Yurts : living in the round / Becky Kemery. – 1st ed.
        p. cm.
    Includes bibliographical references and index.
    ISBN 1-58685-891-2   ISBN 13: 978-1-58685-891-9
    1. Yurts. I. Title.

TH4870.K46 2006
690'.8–dc22

2006012170

CONTENTS

ACKNOWLEDGMENTS

Any project like this involves a journey, and this journey has been made with the support and assistance of a large community.

One of the greatest joys has been meeting and interviewing the visionaries behind the modern yurt movement; each is an inspiration. I met Alan Bair and Pete Dolan of Pacific Yurts while working as a tradeshow carpenter, before I ever thought of writing this book. I was impressed with Alan's work from the start–from the design elements he instigated and the company he created to his unwavering commitment to opening up the market through every possible avenue. Pete Dolan, responsible for the legendary customer service of Pacific Yurts, has helped with many aspects of the book, from assisting with photo collection to providing advice, and along with Alan reviewing sections of the manuscript. Thank you, Peter and Alan.

Yurt-builder and designer David Raitt, his wife, Kelly, and Annie Raitt all opened their hearts and homes to me, adding their support and many ideas to the project. I've resisted telling David's story in full in this volume since he is writing his own book. A wonderful communicator, David is the best person to share his amazing tale. His book will be a welcome addition to the growing body of literature on yurts.

Dan Neumeyer has helped with this project in more ways than I can recount. He arranged and was present for my initial interview with Bill Coperthwaite in Maine. He has contributed many of the wonderful photographs in the "Ancient Paths" and "Tapered Wall Yurt" chapters, reviewed various chapters, and added his ideas on proportion to Bill's in the "Tapered Wall Yurt" chapter.

Bill Coperthwaite has challenged me to think and live evermore deeply and creatively. Following Bill's example, I've sought to balance each day of writing with what he calls "bread labor"–time spent planting and harvesting and chopping and stacking wood. His ideas constantly challenge me to bring simplicity, joy, and thoughtfulness to everything I do.

Paul King, owner of Woodland Yurts in Somerset, England, author of *The Complete Yurt Handbook*, and a leader in the European yurt movement, contributed many photographs and much encouragement. Thank you, Paul.

Morgan Reiter of Oregon Yurtworks likewise granted interviews, reviewed parts of the manuscript on frame panel yurts, and gave excellent feedback. Thank you, Morgan.

Many other yurt builders and innovators have shared their time and their stories with me. Among them are Kirk Bachman, Chuck and Laurel Cox, Emma and Dan Kiger, Jenny Pell, Will Hayes, brothers Jeff and Bo Norris, Blue Evening Star, Jessica and Lee Tenhoff, Jerry Gray, and Howie Oakes. Those in Europe include Hal Wynne Jones, Steve Place, Charles Leys, Rob Matthews, and Alexandr Spado.

Others who have shared their stories with me include yurt dwellers and those who use yurts in their business or nonprofit endeavors. Many of their stories are included here, others are not, but all who gave interviews or shared information have become part of the fabric of the book. Thank you all.

I am especially grateful to those who enlightened me from their areas of expertise. Jan Sitarz taught me about felting and shared books. Navajo scholar Harry Walters talked with me about the hogan. Sandpoint, Idaho, building inspector Don Carter helped decode the building codes. Teresa Lunde of Horizon Northwest Home Mortgage explored yurt financing with me, and Carol Bethel of Harris Dean Insurance researched my insurance questions. Thank you all for your additions to the book.

To all who reviewed portions of the manuscript and gave feedback–Annick Smith, Bill Coperthwaite, Harry Walters, Maxx Sonadre, David Kraisler, Joseph Wythe, Pat Sparks, Beth and Larry Beede, Rob Matthews, Torvald Faegre, John Cloud, and others– thank you. Yurt-scholar Peter Alford Andrews, in particular, provided detailed feedback on the "Ancient Paths" chapter, which greatly enriched the content. Many of the North American yurt companies also gave their input on the "Modern Fabric Yurt" chapter, making corrections and adding needed information. Thank you all. At points of conflicting information, I have made choices to the best of my ability; mistakes that remain in the book are my responsibility.

People from around the world generously shared their yurt photos with me–again many more than could be included–and I thank you all. Scott Vlaun, gifted photographer and writer, stepped forward to take additional photographs of the frame panel yurts. His photographs grace the back jacket of this book and much of the last two chapters. Thanks so much, Scott, for your commitment to this project and for maintaining the highest standards in everything you do.

Others who have made major photographic contributions include Bill Coperthwaite, Peter Alford Andrews, Peter Forbes, and Beth and Larry Beede.

Thank you, Torvald Faegre, for drawing maps and diagrams for the book. It was good to have your involvement in the project.

Zizi Vlaun, thank you for your design work on the Web site www.yurtinfo.org, which preceded this book and brought lots of additional connections and information my way.

I've received writing support from many quarters over the years. Many thanks to the fabulous writers in my online writing group of 2002 for support early in the game, and in particular to Wendy Orange and the Bassar Arts Foundation for a research grant to study yurts. Thank you, Catherine Wanek, for your ongoing guidance and mentoring. Thanks to Heather MacElwain and Zach Hagadone for their careful editing input, and to my current writing group, the North Idaho Writers' Collective, for continuing support.

One of the wonderful things about living in a small town is that a project like this becomes a community affair. Many friends and neighbors have helped in various ways. Special thanks go to Joyce Jowdy and Maggie Abrahmson for assistance with photo collection and Virginia Schmidt for help with photo selection.

The East Bonner County Public Library has provided immense help and support, in particular through the work of Peggy Lanaville and Carol

Holmquist, who retrieved numerous volumes for me through the Interlibrary Loan Department, and Gina Emory who provided frequent technical assistance. Thanks also to the architecture library at University of Washington, an important resource in the area of vernacular architecture.

To baristas and local coffee shops everywhere, home of the itinerant writer, thank you–especially Monarch Mountain Coffee, Common Knowledge Bookstore and Teahouse, and Coldwater Creek Coffeeshop in Sandpoint, Idaho.

Thank you, Philip Freddolino, for helping me build my yurt platform, install my stove, sponge paint my floor, and insulate my yurt. Thanks for being my ongoing technical resource and friend.

It is the publisher that makes a book like this even a remote possibility for an author. My deepest gratitude goes to Suzanne Taylor, Madge Baird, and everyone at Gibbs Smith, Publisher for having the vision to take on this project and the patience to see it through. Many thanks to my editor, Aimee Stoddard, for her loving care of the manuscript, and to Leticia Le Bleu for her careful work with the photographs. Special thanks to Steve Rachwal for his gorgeous book design.

My biggest supporters through this entire project have been my parents, Peter and Evelyn Kemery. They visited me in my very first rental yurt and shared my delight in its beauty. They watched me buy my first yurt and helped me buy the second. They have been a part of this project in ways that no one will see, from financial support and manuscript feedback to German translation work–as well as just pure friendship and support. It wouldn't have been the same journey without you, Mom and Dad. Thank you so much!

FOREWORD

It is with great pleasure that I find this
long-awaited study of yurts ready for the press.

For me, the native yurt is a wonderful symbol of the folk genius of the nomads in inner Asia. Somewhere in the dawn of prehistory these wandering peoples realized they could raise a tipi onto a folding lattice wall and hold it together with a girdle, a rope, a tension band, eliminating the clutter of struts, guy ropes, and poles and gaining greatly in clear, open space. This was the work of many minds over many years. The crowning glory of the design was the tension band.

While there are many small differences in yurt design as you move from tribe to tribe across the high, dry country of central Asia, the basic design of the yurt remains the same: a portable dwelling consisting of a folding lattice wall and radial roof poles set in a skylight rim, all held together with a tension band at the eaves and the whole covered with thick blankets of wool felt. The design has reached such a pinnacle of perfection that it is extremely difficult to imagine improving on it using only materials available to the nomadic herders. The yurt was a brilliant solution to the shelter needs of these peoples. Its genius is on a par with the Eskimo kayak, the lapstrake boats of Scandinavia, the trulli domes of Alberobello, and the instruments of Cremona.

It is from deep admiration for this native design wisdom that I chose to call the modern structures derived from it *yurts* (a Tatar word for house, now in general use replacing myriad tribal terms). The elements my yurts have in common with the native ones include a central round skylight surrounded by a circular building and held together by a tension band. A native yurt would not fare well on the Maine coast where I live (and the price of all that handmade felt–in muscle or coin–would be formidable). Likewise, modern wooden yurts would be ridiculous for a people who must move with their herds, not to mention that wood is a scarce material in their region.

My work with yurt design has not focused so much on the search for better housing as on the search for better ways to live. The modern yurt is a beautiful example of cultural blending–of borrowing structural principles from Central Asian nomads and blending these with modern materials. If we are to discover, design, and create healthy ways for humans to interact with their home–this oasis in a galactic desert–we must take cultural blending to heart and glean what wisdom we can from all of our neighbors on this planet.

WILLIAM S. COPERTHWAITE
Originator of the tapered wall yurt
Director, the Yurt Foundation
Author, *A Handmade Life*

PREFACE

It rests on a deck that took a couple of weeks to build, but only because we were clearing land and planting a garden at the same time.

At night, I fall asleep looking up through a round central skylight at diamonds speckling an inky black sky. If I'm lucky, coyotes sing the moon up and on its path, and, if the angle is right, an escaped moonbeam might slide through the skylight circle and across my floor. A nearby creek washes its soundscape through my dreams, and birdsong wakes me for my morning tea.

Yurt living has been my habit for awhile now. This is the fourth yurt I've lived in, and the second that I've owned. It's my shelter of choice. I love the open feel, the graceful lift of the roof, and the encircling roundness. I love being close to nature and my surroundings. Not everybody likes to live in one large room, but it suits me just fine. In the summer, I use an outdoor kitchen to cook for friends, dry herbs from my garden, and make huckleberry jam. In the winter, soup simmers on the woodstove that heats the yurt and morning coffee percolates on a small 1950s propane stove rescued from a trailer.

In many respects, this book is about design, about taking an ancient, time-tested, and worthy design from an indigenous culture and exploring the ways it can be stretched to meet a broad cross section of contemporary needs. Throughout the book you'll hear the voices of what yurt-builder David Raitt calls "imagineers," gifted people thinking outside the box of modern concepts of shelter. Some of them clothe the ancient forms in modern materials, while others express their design philosophies through unusual expansions of the form itself.

The first chapter, "What's a Yurt?," looks at what defines a yurt, the mechanics of its circular architecture and its unique characteristics. Today, we not only have the womblike indigenous Central Asian yurts, the Turkic üy and Mongolian ger, but also three modern versions. This chapter defines the distinctive features of these five types of shelter that are all called "yurts" and outlines their history. The rest of that history unfolds in stories and sidebars woven throughout the book.

Not everyone wants to modify yurt design. The first chapter also tells the story of yurt makers in the UK and European Union who have chosen to stay close to the ancient, time-tested designs of Central Asia, with occasional modifications to accommodate climatic variables. In countries with deep historical roots and centuries-old buildings, the style of the ancient yurts seems more appropriate. Innovation has come mainly in their varied uses.

Yurts are one of the oldest indigenous forms of

architecture, carrying the energy of tribal nomads crossing the Asian steppes from millennia past. "Ancient Paths," the second chapter, explores the origins of these nomad homes and their use during the period of the great Mongol Khans, when yurt dwellers conquered and ruled the largest empire in history. This chapter also clarifies the two distinct designs that have evolved along tribal lines and explains how these yurts are made, transported, and erected. The Mongolian understanding of "home" as sacred space is described, along with lessons the yurt brings us from the unique perspective of the nomad.

As described in chapter three, the "Tapered Wall Yurt," yurts came to North America through the passion and vision of Bill Coperthwaite, a lifelong student of indigenous design and tribal technologies and a teacher of "democratic social design." Bill retained the nomads' philosophy of simplicity, self-sufficiency, and connection to the natural world while modifying yurt design to use local materials and meet the need of North Americans for permanent shelter. His tapered wall yurts are rustic as well as beautiful in design and proportion.

One of the most stunning tapered wall yurts is the three-tiered yurt with a cupola that is Bill Coperthwaite's home and the home of the Yurt Foundation, a repository for worldwide indigenous crafts and design. Located on four hundred acres in Maine and bordered by the seacoast on one side and forested woodlands on the other, it stands as a symbol of the melding of ancient and modern and of the beauty and magic that are possible when the human heart expresses itself in intelligent design. The third chapter also tells the stories of two families who built their own tapered wall yurt homes, one family using Bill's plans and the other creating their own design.

North Americans tend to think of yurts as the fabric-covered, trellis-walled structures they see in parks or stay in while skiing backcountry trails. The portable, flexible modern fabric yurt, with its extraordinary range of uses from homes and classrooms to bed and breakfasts, is the subject of chapter four, the "Modern Fabric Yurt." A fabric yurt, more comfortable than a tent but still not quite a house, is different from what most of us are accustomed to for shelter. This chapter answers the most frequently asked questions about living in fabric yurts—from foundations, heating and bathrooms, to bears and building codes. You'll also see a lot of examples of how people have used fabric yurts for business, pleasure, and as homes.

Chapter five, the "Frame Panel Yurt," looks at a design that has combined elements of conventional stick-frame building with prefab innovation to take the yurt and circular design to new and unusual places. The designers of the frame panel yurt set out to provide affordable permanent homes that are custom designed to meet the needs of individual families. In frame panel yurts, the concept of circular living expands to include contemporary, luxurious, multistory structures with rectilinear connectors and uses ranging from homes to office buildings and churches. This

MY REASON FOR WRITING THIS BOOK IS SIMPLE: YURTS ARE MY FAVORITE FORM OF SHELTER. THEY USE THE EARTH'S RESOURCES WISELY AND USUALLY LEAVE A SMALL FOOTPRINT. THEY ARE AFFORDABLE AND ACCESSIBLE. I ALSO THINK THEY MAKE FABULOUS SPIRITUAL AND CREATIVE SPACES.

chapter shows a cross section of examples and includes an architect's perspective on circular design.

The last chapter examines what "Living in the Round" means in terms of the interior use of circular space. A yurt dweller has many options, ranging from built-in rooms and lofts to outbuildings and satellite yurts. This chapter provides pictures and floor plans to demonstrate the broad range of possibilities available in working with circular spaces.

The appendixes contain additional tools for the fabric yurt dweller, including excerpts from building codes and a sample platform plan and woodstove and chimney diagrams.

The Resource Guide contains listings of yurt companies, yurt plans, books, films, Web sites, and online forums. Updated listings and a yurt newsletter can be found on the Web site www.yurtinfo.org.

My reason for writing this book is simple: yurts are my favorite form of shelter. They use the earth's resources wisely and usually leave a small footprint. They are affordable and accessible. I also think they make fabulous spiritual and creative spaces.

My favorite yurt was in Oregon's Cascade Mountains on the Breitenbush River. A meandering woodland path led from the front door to a pair of Adirondack chairs at the river's edge. The floor of the yurt was made of cob (a mixture of clay, sand, and straw similar to adobe). Hot springs water, carried by pipes in the floor, warmed my feet and the yurt through long snowy winters. Shimmering sheer fabric hung across the foot of my bed, creating a sense of privacy without cutting off the yurt's spacious uplift. On the opposite side of the yurt, an air mattress on the warm floor welcomed myriad overnight guests.

The yurt was a natural gathering place for community functions, with everything from business meetings to a South African spice ritual held within its gracious, enfolding space. Some nights I'd light a raft of candles and friends would gather to play music and sing. Dancers stepped and twirled under the skylight in the middle. One night we counted over twenty people singing, dancing, and watching from pillows around the perimeter. Would those gatherings have held the same magic in the boxy buildings most of us call home? I don't know. I do know that I'm not the only one who finds in yurts a special kind of space.

I hope this book conveys something of the beauty, and the magic, of these round shelters.

WHAT'S A YURT?

"The true basis for the more serious study of the art of architecture lies with those indigenous more humble buildings everywhere, that are to architecture what folklore is to literature, or folksong to music...Functions are truthfully conceived and rendered invariably with natural feeling. Results are often beautiful and always instructive."

—Frank Lloyd Wright, *A Testament*

Karie Knoke needed a house but didn't have time to build one. A computer-systems designer turned commercial fisher, Karie spent her summers living aboard a boat and trolling for salmon in the fjords and inlets of southeast Alaska. When the fishing season ended, she had only two or three months at home before it started to snow–not much time to pour a foundation and build a house.

After researching various housing options, Karie ordered a yurt. It was a beautiful wine-colored fabric yurt, thirty feet in diameter, with large windows and a full insulation package. The site on which she chose to locate her yurt was close to a rushing river and had a view of mountains across the river.

Karie built a tall yurt platform. "I wanted the deck eight feet off the ground," she said, "so that I could have a large, enclosed space for firewood and storage underneath the yurt and could put the woodstove there if I wanted to." The cedar logs holding up the platform came from the river, already peeled and de-limbed by nature. Karie used her truck to pull them out of the riverbed and up the bank.

From the mountain steppes of Central Asia to this modern guesthouse in Los Angeles, the yurt provides a form of shelter that is affordable, simple to erect, and eminently livable.

When the deck was finished, Karie called together friends for a yurt-raising party. Fifteen showed up, armed with generators and power tools. "There were more tools than we needed," Karie said. "The yurt went up in a day and a half. The extra half day was required because the deck was so high that much of the work had to be done on ladders, which took a lot longer."

Now, three years later, Karie reflects on her space. "I love the yurt," she says. "Everything has been great, aside from the time when a bear climbed up onto the deck joists and tore into the fabric, trying to get into the yurt. (Our river drainage has been called a bear superhighway, so I guess it's not surprising.) The bear wasn't able to get in and my yurt company sent me fabric to repair the tear. Other than that incident, it's been a wonderful living space."

DEFINING A YURT

Most yurts are portable, tent-like structures. They have circular lattice walls (reminiscent of baby gates tied together) and a cone-shaped roof supported by rafters that meet in a center ring. The outer fabric shell of the yurt can be made of felted wool, coated canvas, or a modern architectural fabric.

An ever-increasing number of wooden structures are also called yurts. What defines them as yurts and not just round houses? The answer lies in the yurt's uncommon roof structure.

The yurt roof incorporates a unique architectural design. Roof struts meet in a center ring, producing inward and downward pressure. This center ring holds the rafters in a state of compression. Where the struts meet the wall at the perimeter, a natural outward thrust occurs. A band (of rope, woven

"My yurt is my cocoon and my temple," says fisherwoman Karie Knoke. Despite the convenience of having a winter's supply of wood stacked under the yurt, Karie isn't sure she would build a tall deck again. "I enjoy the view and hanging out with the trees," she says, "but the high platform makes it difficult to feel grounded and connected with the earth."

Not all yurts are portable. Wooden yurts, which were inspired by the original yurt designs and use the same roof architecture, provide permanent living and work spaces. This tapered wall concentric yurt in North Carolina includes a small, raised interior yurt that shares the main roof and provides additional floor space.

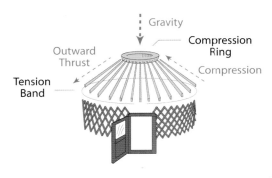

Gravity

Outward Thrust

Compression Ring

Compression

Tension Band

Various forces operate on a yurt roof. Gravity pulls down on the roof struts, creating an outward thrust against the outer wall and a force of compression against the inner ring. The roof struts are held in a state of tension between the compression ring at the center and the tension band at the top of the wall. This gives the yurt roof its unique combination of flexibility and strength.

cloth, or wire cable) at the top of the wall holds the wall and roof poles in tension against this outward pressure.

Because of this combination of a central compression ring at the top of the roof and the encircling tension band where the roof meets the wall, long roof spans are possible without any internal support system (like posts, trusses, or beams). This gives the yurt an uncommon feeling of spaciousness and uplift. The roof design also creates an incredibly strong and resilient structure that is uniquely equipped to withstand earthquakes, strong winds, and heavy snow loads.

ANCESTORS: THE CENTRAL ASIAN YURTS

Yurts originated in the high mountain steppes of Central Asia. No one knows exactly where the first yurt came from or how it was invented.

Nomadic tribes in Europe and Asia have used round structures for millennia. From the huts of Finnish reindeer herders to the benders of Turkic nomads and Siberian tipis, most nomadic shelters have been either domed or conical in shape. The yurt has taken these round nomad shelters a step

The Siberian *yaranga* has a raised tipi-style roof that rests on tripod stands. Covered with reindeer skins, this possible precursor to the yurt is still used by reindeer herders in Siberia and northern Mongolia.

farther by placing the dome or cone on a trellis wall, thereby creating a more spacious, livable structure that maintains all of the benefits of the circle.

Following the conquests of Chingiz Khan (Genghis Khan) and the rise of the Mongol empire in the thirteenth century, use of the yurt spread across Asia, the Middle East, and parts of Europe. The Magyar people of Hungary, who claim the yurt as part of their heritage, are evidence of the broad reach of the yurt since the time of the Mongol empire.

In the seventeenth and eighteenth centuries, explorers traversed Central Asia and Siberia, leaving behind detailed accounts of yurts and the daily life of the nomads who lived in them. From their accounts, we know that not much has changed in yurt design or nomadic habits over the past few hundred years.

Two current versions of Central Asian yurts have developed along tribal lines. Although basically the same structure, the Turkic üy and Mongolian ger differ in a number of respects. Differences include the shape of the roof struts, the design of the central ring, and the style of the doors. While the Mongolians use only felted outer coverings and leave them undecorated, some of the Turkic tribes add decorative work to both felted coverings and reed walls.

The original yurt design provided a shelter ideally suited to nomadic life. In a land without trees, it had a lightweight framework of willow, made to last a lifetime and easy to transport. The felted outer covering was made on-site from the wool of sheep close at hand. An average-sized yurt could be transported on the backs of two camels and set up or taken down in as little as thirty minutes.

Little has changed over the centuries in the design of the Central Asian shepherd's home. With walls that can be folded up and a covering made from sheep's wool, the original yurt is easy to transport and can be set up in as little as thirty minutes. The Turkic version of the yurt, the üy, has bentwood roof poles, a lightweight center ring, and a door flap. Some of the Turkic yurts, like these festival yurts in Kirghizstan, are highly decorated.

The Mongolian version of the yurt, called the ger, with straight roof poles and a heavy, decorative door.

"For nomads, very simply, there exists the everyday necessity of living in harmony with nature, otherwise they can't survive — and this situation never changes."

—WHERE HORSES FLY LIKE THE WIND,
Silk Road film series

"The yurt is a simple artifact derived by generations of people living life their way. They have given this to the world and our responsibility is to see that we respect it in our adaptations and utilization. We must honor and respect those who gave us the beauty, elegance, and sheer simplicity that is the strength of the yurt. Acting in this spirit we cannot go wrong. How we go about this is the challenge we face."

—Rob Matthews, yurt builder

Across cultures and through the ages, the circle remains a symbol of the unity of all things, the wholeness of life with all its interconnections. Rectilinear structures naturally separate and compartmentalize, fitting things neatly into square rooms and boxes. The yurt, as a circular structure, has the potential to bring things together again, to make things whole, to call us back to our connection with nature and with life in its entirety. The yurt makes its contribution to the modern shelter design both as a circular structure and in its connection to the indigenous people who birthed the design.

The early yurt dwellers teach us to see shelter as sacred space. Everything in the yurt is oriented to the four directions, and in this way the yurt provides a physical compass for the nomad. It also provides a spiritual compass, a constant reminder of connection to the world beneath the sacred central fire, the heavens above the smoke hole, and the duality of surrounding life with its yin and yang, or masculine and feminine, principles, which must be held in tension and balance. The knowledge that the nomads hold of their place in the world and their intimate connection to it is at the core of a way of life so sustainable that they have lived for thousands of years in a delicate land without upsetting the balance or leaving a trace behind them.

As a nomadic culture, the original yurt dwellers also pass on the gifts of simplicity, of distilling life into few possessions, and of the intimacy of family, tribe, and relationship with the surrounding natural world.

The yurt, in all its modern variants, is still intimately connected to the ancient cultures of the indigenous nomad. Through this connection, the yurt brings gifts far beyond its function as a beautiful and comfortable shelter. Almost all the inventors and builders of the modern yurt recognize and associate to some degree with aspects of the original indigenous values and culture.

MODERN YURT DESIGN

North American innovators have pushed yurt design parameters from the start, providing us with three new, unique designs: the tapered wall yurt; the modern fabric yurt, which maintains the portable trellis wall of the Central Asian design; and the frame panel yurt.

The Tapered Wall Yurt

Bill Coperthwaite is a brilliant and inspiring educator who uses yurt-building workshops as a tool to help people rethink their relationship with the natural world and see themselves as designers of their own better world. He chose the yurt for his design exploration because of its natural strength, beauty, and simplicity. While promoting the indigenous values behind the yurt (simplicity, self-sufficiency, and connection to the natural world), he created a permanent structure using locally viable materials. The Central Asian yurts developed in a land where wood was scarce and wool plentiful. In North America, where wool is precious and wood is plentiful, Bill's yurts are built of wood.

This tapered wall yurt in Alaska was built in the 1960s in a workshop led by Bill Coperthwaite. Following in the footsteps of the original yurts, this permanent yurt uses a locally abundant building material (in this case, wood).

Many of Bill's tapered wall yurts are rustic, meaning they sometimes are not insulated and may not be as mouse proof as a conventional house. The outwardly slanting walls can also present challenges for incorporating storage and furniture into the yurt. At the same time, the tapered walls make for great seating, the yurts are attractive and light filled, and many people find them to be delightful living spaces. Their greatest advantage is that the plans are simple enough for almost anyone to build.

The Modern Fabric Yurt

Chuck and Laurel Cox, a couple of Bill Coperthwaite's students, drew up an initial set of plans for the modern fabric yurt, based on the Mongolian ger. These plans became the basis for most of the homebuilt and commercial designs that followed.

Alan Bair and his company Pacific Yurts kept many of the original structural elements from the Coxes' plans but modified both materials and aesthetics to align the yurt with contemporary North American sensibilities. The encircling rope tension band is made of steel aircraft cable sitting neatly on top of the lattice wall. The latest in modern architectural fabrics have replaced the outer covering of felted wool or coated canvas, and NASA-developed insulation provides lightweight but effective temperature control. An acrylic skylight bubble and multiple windows create a light-filled and spacious interior.

The modern fabric yurt moves beyond the merely functional with custom colors, multiple windows, and an acrylic skylight bubble. These two yurts function as kitchen and classroom at a Canyonlands Field Institute campus near Moab, Utah.

The Frame Panel Yurt

When David Raitt, another of Bill Coperthwaite's students, evolved designs for frame panel yurts, he was looking at sustainability and shelter through very practical lenses. Most North Americans want a structure that is mouse proof and airtight, but they have neither the time nor expertise to build the structure themselves—the learning curve is too high. In the frame panel yurt, the round shape of the yurt and the spacious architecture of the yurt roof are maintained, and the yurt is transformed into a permanent stick-frame structure prefabricated off-site and put together by a crew on location in a matter of days. The prefabricated panels include insulation and are finished on the inside. The owner can do the exterior finish and systems work (electrical, plumbing, and so on) or it can be contracted out.

Frame panel design covers a wide spectrum from small one-room guest cottages, like this one, to workshop spaces and professional offices. The stick-frame panels are prefabricated off-site and then put together by an on-site crew in a matter of days.

HONORING THE ANCIENT TRADITIONS

Not all modern builders want to modify the original yurt design. Members of organizations like the Society for Creative Anachronism (SCA) build their own yurts based on both Turkic and Mongolian designs. Primarily a historical exercise, these yurts tend to be rustic and are used primarily for annual reenactment gatherings.

In Europe (where it's not uncommon to live in a five-hundred-year-old house), the European love of history and authenticity is reflected in their

Society of Creative Anachronism (SCA) member Bill Lubarsky built this yurt to use at reenactment events, where he is identified as Avrahm ben Aharon of the Dragonship Haven.

approach to yurts. Why change an ancient design that has worked so well for thousands of years? "We stick to the Mongolian sizes and principles," says Rob Matthews of the Yurt Workshop in Andalucia, Spain. "We believe that three thousand years of experience needs no discussion."

Key influences in the European yurt movement include English builder Paul King's book *The Complete Yurt Handbook* and a set of Turkic yurt plans by Welshman Steve Place.[1] Hal Wynne-Jones of Turkoman Yurts in Gloucester, England, has taught some of Europe's finest yurt builders. One interesting structural innovation is Wynne-Jones's composite multiplex Turkic yurt, which he rents out for weddings and events.

The European yurts are extremely portable, like their Central Asian counterparts, and they have found their way into a number of unique situations. They have been used by alternative groups to create nomadic yurt communities, and by political activists as temporary shelters during demonstrations.[2] Many yurt builders rent out yurts for events. Felters have used yurts as an art medium. Yurts have also been used in educational work with children.[3]

The multiplex yurt, built by Englishman Hal Wynne-Jones, is based on the Turkic design with bentwood roof struts. The yurt is used as a rental for weddings, festivals, and other events.

The Storytelling Yurt is made of twelve felted panels, four feet wide by seven feet high. Each panel contains at least one tree and woodland wildlife animal, and the roof of the yurt is a felted sky. A collaborative project of Scottish and Irish felters, with some panels contributed by California felters, the yurt was originally designed for a 1999 felting exhibition in Glasgow, Scotland. Today, it functions as a nomadic learning center, traveling to schools and festivals around the UK.

YURT CRAFTING IN EUROPE

Yurt builders in the UK and European Union lovingly reproduce by hand the Central Asian designs, both Mongolian and Turkic. The only significant structural difference is an expanded spacing of the trellis components (and therefore also the roof struts) from six or seven inches in the Central Asian design to about twelve inches in the European versions.[4]

Most European yurt makers use coated canvas for their outer covering, while a few use architectural fabrics. Some recommend the Central Asian practice of using felted wool, sandwiched between an inner cotton layer and outer canvas layer for rain protection.

Most yurt makers in the UK make their structural components with sawn timber from the ash tree, but some use coppiced poles. Coppicing, which produces a large number of good, straight poles, involves cutting an established tree like willow, chestnut, or ash down at the base. New shoots grow from the base and can be harvested every three or four years for yurt poles.

ABOVE: (CLOCKWISE FROM TOP LEFT) French yurt artisan Charles Leys sews a yurt cover; Rob Matthews of the Yurt Workshop in Andalucia, Spain, crafts a Mongolian center ring, or crown; completed crowns at the Yurtworks workshop in Cornwall, England; a crown made by Steve Place of Handmade Hardwood Yurts in Wales; Charles Leys burns holes in a Kirghiz yurt crown.

LEFT: (CLOCKWISE FROM LEFT) A French yurt in residence at a chateau; a rooftop yurt in Spain; a holiday yurt in Cornwall, England; yurts, built by Englishman Paul King, at a fair; and a snowy scene in the Czech Republic with a yurt built by Alexandr Spado of Workshop Under the Hill.

THE SPECIAL MAGIC OF YURTS

"Circular living provides a balance of looking inward and outward, looking out at the natural environment and surroundings but then coming in again to the self and the hearth."

–David Raitt, yurt builder

Yurts have many tangible advantages. The circular floor plan provides the greatest amount of space possible for the materials used. A round space is also the most efficient space to heat and leaves the least amount of exterior surface area exposed to the elements. Wind naturally moves around yurts, instead of getting caught at corners. Because of their engineering and roof structures, yurts are extraordinarily strong, withstanding earthquakes, high winds, and heavy snow loads.

The rounded yurt fits into its natural surroundings more readily than rectilinear buildings, and the Central Asian and fabric yurts leave a small footprint. The fabric yurts also provide a healthy option for people with chemical sensitivities because of the less-toxic materials used and the more frequent air exchange that occurs.

BELOW: Yurts fit well into the natural surroundings. This yurt combines the profile of the tapered wall yurt with frame panel prefabrication. The many windows reinforce the connection between the inside and the wooded surroundings.

FACING: "You come inside the yurt to the self and the hearth," says builder David Raitt, "and the skylight draws you up."

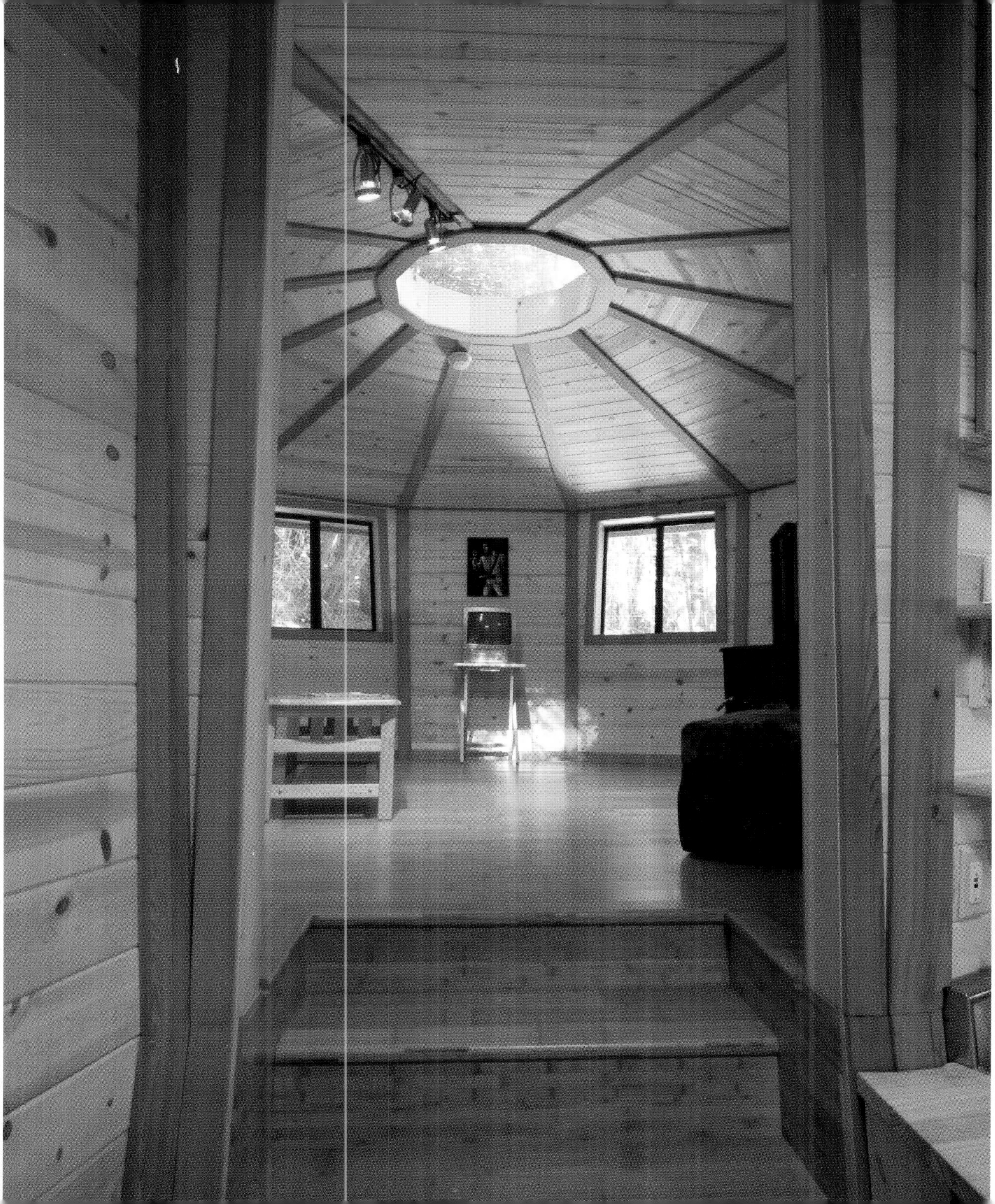

Yurts can be found at many retreat centers. This frame panel yurt at Breitenbush Hot Springs Retreat and Conference Center in Oregon originally housed a pool for WATSU hydrotherapy. Today, it is a comfortable workshop space.

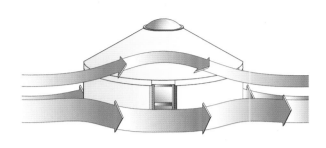

One of the tangible advantages of yurts is that there are no corners to catch the wind, which naturally flows over and around the yurt.

The healing, creative, communal, and spiritual nature of yurts is broadly recognized. Yurts seem especially suited to certain pursuits. They are often used in retreat centers and for the healing arts, meditation, spiritual practices, dancing, and community gatherings. People seem to sleep better in yurts, and they often dream more.

It is ultimately the intangibles that sell people on yurts. Morgan Reiter, founder of Oregon Yurtworks, says that the tangible advantages "make the sale less than 10 percent of the time. People buy yurts because of the special feeling they experience when they are in a yurt, and all the rest is icing on the cake."

Wherever it is found, and whatever form it takes, the well-made yurt is a gift to those privileged to live or work in one. This ancient nomadic shelter, which provides a reprieve from the rectilinear excesses of modern culture, reminds us through its circular form of the unity and interconnectedness of all things. Versatile and beautiful, both ancient and contemporary versions provide shelter that is affordable, accessible, and gentle to the earth.

For many, the yurt is simply a delightful space in which to wrap oneself and spend some time. But if we can hear it, the yurt also whispers to us–through the millennia–to follow in the footsteps of nomadic cultures and live with simplicity, in balance, and in harmony with the planet.

"People are very much affected by these structures, whether they are modern Americans or an indigenous person on the steppes of Central Asia. There's the primordial and spiritual and community appeal of living in a round structure, with its connection to our ancient roots. There's also the quality of the space itself. With its embracing walls and its open-at-the-top architecture, it is both a protective and soothing space and a symbol of the metaphysical quality of being open and receptive to what life has to bring you. It has a very positive impact on the people who come into contact with it."

–Annie Raitt, cofounder of California Yurts

ANCIENT PATHS
THE CENTRAL ASIAN ÜY AND GER

"As we face the challenges of the disharmony we've created for ourselves, we must regain this ancient and everlasting wisdom in order to create solutions that truly work for us, the larger family of life around us, and for seven generations of children."

—Brooke Medicine Eagle, *Simply Living*

Many centuries ago, long before the time of Mohammed, Buddha, or Christ, a people with oak-colored skin and almond eyes rode their horses and camels across grasslands at the top of the world. These nomads followed herds of sheep, goats, and yak through wind-swept steppes bounded by enormous jagged peaks.

Agriculture wasn't practicable in this arid land of bitter extremes, and trees were scarce. Only by developing a reciprocal relationship with their domestic animals were the herders able to survive in this harsh near-desert environment. Even then, to keep their flocks fed they had to move constantly in cycle with the seasons.

Each day members of the family took their flocks of sheep or goats to fresh pasture, just beyond the previous day's journey. Every evening they returned home and the animals huddled together near the herders' round shelters. When the distance to new pasture grew beyond a day's journey, the people moved with their flocks to new grazing grounds, beginning again the journey outward to fresh pasture.

Yurts are one of the oldest forms of indigenous shelter still used today by nomads from Turkey to Mongolia.

When the days grew short and a chill hung in the air, the herders packed their belongings onto horses and carts and moved to lower elevations. There they settled into hospitable valleys that sheltered their flocks from the bitter winds of a winter interminably long and cold beyond imagining. In their round shelters, the herders gathered around the fire to drink fermented mares' milk. They shared stories, made music, and recited poems through the long winter nights. With the arrival of spring, they again moved up to the mountains, to fresh green grasslands where their animals grew fat and strong and had babies, continuing the cycle of life.

The same flocks provided not only food but also clothes and fuel for the family. Milk, cheese, and yogurt were mainstays of the people's diet, and fermented mares' milk was their alcohol. They made sheep's wool into garments and camel, yak, and goat hair into belts. Each morning the children of the household went to the pen and gathered dung left by the flocks; this they dried for fire fuel.

The animals also provided materials for shelter. The herders constructed lattice walls from willow saplings and pinned them together with strips of rawhide. They tied the lattice sections in a circle, using rope or woven bands made from wool and

The flocks of the Central Asian nomad provide food, clothing, and shelter. The collapsible structural elements of the nomad's shelter, made from willow rods or sawn lumber, are meant to last a lifetime. The felted outer covering, made from sheep's wool, can be replaced as needed with wool from the flocks at hand.

horsehair. Over the wooden framework of the lattice walls and a circular roof, they placed an outer covering of felt (made from sheep's wool spread in layers, sprinkled with water, and formed into mats).

From ancient times, the herders lived in small family units within larger tribal groups that shared language, culture, and religious traditions. Their beliefs acknowledged the sacredness of all things and the need to keep balance between the material world and the realms above and below. They also sought to keep in balance the culture of people and the world of nature. Everything they did reflected this belief.

ANCIENT BEGINNINGS

In the vast landmass that is Central Asia, two tribal groupings have remained distinct. The Turkic tribes wandered over the stretch of continent from Iran in the west to China in the east.[1] The Mongolian tribes, which are thought to have originated in the Buryat region of Siberia, ranged from the Siberian regions of Buryatia and Tuva in the north, through Mongolia, and south to the Inner Mongolia region of China.

When did these tribes begin using the yurt? No one really knows. Some scholars believe Turkic tribes used the yurt in the middle of the first millennium AD. Other scholars have traced it back further to the Scytho-Sakian era (eighth to third century BC).[2] We do know, from archeological findings of both felted objects and wooden wheels, that the technology required for making yurts was well developed by the fifth century BC.[3]

The lack of early archeological evidence isn't surprising. Nomads don't leave behind buildings, monuments, or libraries. Their perishable wood and felt dwellings are erected directly on the ground and then moved from encampment to encampment. Nomads also put every part of the yurt–from felts to structural components–to use for other purposes when they are no longer useful as shelter.[4]

According to the oral traditions of the tribes themselves, the yurt's connection to tribal identity dates back even further. The Gokleng Turkmen of Iran, for example, claim that the prophet Nuh (Noah) created the yurt. Near Eastern historian Mirkhwand, writing in the late fifteenth century, echoed this idea when he proposed that the yurt was invented by Noah's grandson Turk, son of Japheth.[5]

The Chinese poet Po Chu-I, writing between AD 829 and 846, provided the first actual word picture in a poem describing his own yurt:

The fine fleece from a thousand sheep is brought together;
Hundreds of arcs are fitted together tautly,
The round skeleton and the willow staves of the sides
    are strong.
It is dyed fresh in the dark blue of the northeastern sky.
Made in the north, assembled by tribesmen
It came south in the train of barbarian prisoners.
Even the strongest wind is unable to move it
And it is most stoutly resistant to the rain.
It has a roof rising to a point in the middle;
It has no corners, and is round in the four directions.
A door opens widely in its side;
Inside it is comfortable and warm . . .
It is especially suitable when the ground is covered in frost;
It might well be called a sky amidst the snow. . . .
My guests are received there;
My descendants will hand it on.
The families of princes may boast of their antiquities,
But these do not equal my blue felt![6]

Also writing in the ninth century in the Middle East, al-Ya'qubi wrote about the Turkic tribes: "These Turks have neither refuges at halting places nor strongholds. They only pitch Turkish domes, which are ribbed, and the nails are strips from the hides of pack animals and cattle, and the coverings are felt."[7]

The yurt might have remained an obscure shelter, used by scattered nomadic tribes and virtually unknown to the rest of the world, had it not been for the birth of a shepherd in 1162 into a family of royal heritage but humble means.

Ninth-century writer al-Ya'qubi described the early Turkic yurt when he wrote, "These Turks have neither refuge at halting places nor strongholds. They only pitch Turkish domes [top image], which are ribbed [middle image], and the nails are strips from the hides of pack animals and cattle [bottom left image]." The lattice wall is held together with rawhide strips drawn through holes in the lattice slats, knotted and dried, "and the coverings are felt [bottom right image]."

THE MONGOLIAN EMPIRE

The Secret History of the Mongols, composed around 1228, describes the life of the shepherd Temujin as a young man who was working hard to unite scattered, warring Mongol tribes.[8] Temujin had an unconventional leadership style: he killed the opposition and then offered everyone else a choice–to join and follow, with absolute obedience and allegiance, or die. Within a couple of decades, he had united a large nomadic community and amassed an enormous–and very loyal–army.[9]

At a nomadic congress in 1206, Temujin's followers renamed him Chingiz Khan (Genghis Khan, or Universal Lord). He led his armies on horseback across a vast area, conquering or destroying everything in his path and uniting the Turkic tribes within his Mongol army and empire.

For one hundred and fifty years, during the thirteenth and fourteenth centuries, the yurt-dwelling Mongols ruled the largest empire in human history, which stretched a quarter of the way around the planet and encompassed half of the world's population.

It was the portability of Chingiz's army, along with his gifts of organization and military prowess, that enabled him (and his progenitors) to conquer a vast territory within a very short time. The advance guard traveled with only horses, weapons, and felted cloaks that doubled as sleeping bags or tents. These soldiers cleared the country of its inhabitants–killing or conquering everyone they encountered, but they took no plunder.

The larger army, also on horseback, followed behind, destroying or taking as plunder everything in its path.[10] Behind the army proper came the wives and children of the soldiers, along with livestock. They traveled with cart houses (round felt tents on carts) and felt-covered supply carts. Everything was on wheels. Altogether, it was as mobile and efficient an army as had ever navigated the earth.[11]

For one hundred and fifty years the Mongols ruled the largest empire in history, consisting, after Chingiz Kahn's death, of four separate khanates (or kingdoms) that controlled one-fourth of the planet and included half of its population. Numerous dignitaries and emissaries visited the courts of the ruling Khans, and much was written about Mongol culture and rule. A number of writings describe their housing in detail. Giovanni de Piano Carpini recorded one of the most complete descriptions while on a papal mission to Mongolia between 1245 and 1247:

They have round dwelling places made in the manner of tents, out of withies and slender staves. At the very top in the middle they have a round window, through which light enters, and from which the smoke can go out, for they always make the fire in the middle. Moreover the walls and roofs are covered with felt; even the doors are made of felt. Some of these dwellings are large, and some small, according to the rank or insignificance of the people. Some of them can be quickly taken apart and put together again, and are carried on beasts of burden; some cannot be taken apart, and are moved about on carts. Moreover, to move them on a cart, for the smaller ones one ox is sufficient, for the larger ones three, four, or even more, according to the size. Wherever they go, be it to war or anywhere else, they always move them about with them.[12]

The cart houses were used both in war and in peacetime. Their yurt-like frames rested on a bottom wooden ring that allowed them to extend out beyond the cart's two wheels by as much as five feet on either side. The tents were not collapsible, but the entire tent could be lifted off the cart and placed on the ground. A thirteenth-century account described a cart tent so large (twenty feet in diameter) that it took two rows of eleven oxen each to pull the cart.[13] The Mongols preferred white tents over darker colors, and they sometimes saturated the felt of the cart tents with lime or a powder ground from bones to lighten them.

Marco Polo, traveling with his merchant uncles from Venice to the court of Kublai Khan in Beijing around 1275, wrote of the collapsible tents: "They have houses of timber, and cover them with felts, and they are round, and they carry them wherever they go; for they have bound the timber withies so well, and in such an orderly way, that they can be carried easily. And whenever they stretch and pitch their house, the door is always towards the south."[14]

Chinese sources in the northern plains areas of Central Asia mention both collapsible and cart tents, but there's little trace of the ongoing use of cart tents in the south, where mountain passes made carts less suitable.

yurts at court

In 1264, Chingiz Khan's grandson Kublai Khan moved his capital to what is now Beijing, China. There he built a magnificent palace district, the original Forbidden City. The architecture of the palace reflected diverse cultural styles from Arabic to Chinese. At the center of the palace complex was a vast area of nomadic tents.

These yurts, described from court scenes of the Mongol Empire, ranged in size from small tents, ten feet in diameter and six feet high in the center—hardly large enough for two people to sleep in and not tall enough to really stand in, to large, ornately decorated tents that could hold up to a thousand people. The large yurts were rarely moved.

One visitor to the court of Ögödei Khan wrote that "in the summer he would be in the district of Ormugetu; there he had pitched a great trellis tent, which held a thousand people, and which was never struck. The outside was adorned with golden pins and the inside was enclosed with gold brocade. It is called the Sira Ordo."[15]

White felt tents were provided for guests of the court and sometimes were available for rent on the court grounds.[16] Court shamans had their own tent areas. Visiting Christian priests were provided with yurts that functioned as chapels, denoted by a cross at the top.

Some tents were decorated inside and out with ornamental cloth; others had exterior appliqué patterns like those still found on Kazakh yurts. The raised threshold board at the entrance and sometimes the entire door frame were plated in precious metals. All these decorations were indicators of the status and wealth of the owner.

Among the ladies of the court, each wife had

her own tent. Women were responsible for all the tents in their keep, including servants' tents. It remained customary among many Turkic tribes until the twentieth century for wives to keep separate tents when possible.[17]

The ruling khans kept their amassed wealth, along with household goods, in bow-topped carts. The carts were vaulted, like a covered wagon, and were covered with black felt, which had been waterproofed with ewe's milk or tallow.[18] By using these carts for storage, the Mongols were able to amass great wealth and extraordinary treasure without having to build permanent structures.

RETURN TO NOMADISM

The Mongols influenced world culture and art during their time as the ruling power, yet in their own homeland they built little and left few monuments to their empire. Even the rulers' graves remain unmarked, in true nomadic tradition.[19]

Despite their role as rulers of four vast dynasties, the Mongols chose not to settle. Kublai Khan and his court, for example, maintained their yurt village in the Forbidden City during the winter months and continued to pursue a seasonal nomadic rotation for the rest of the year, as Mongol nomads do today.[20]

When the various empires of the Mongols disintegrated during the fourteenth and fifteenth centuries, the Mongol and Turkic tribes separated from each other once again. The Turkic tribes remained in many of the territories into which they had moved and converted to Islam under the influence of the Arabs and Iranians. Most of the Mongols moved back to their ancestral lands and reinstated their nomadic patterns. The Mongols underwent a gradual conversion to Buddhism and became a

This painting from 1793 shows cart tents, collapsible yurts, and felt-covered, bow-topped carts in use on the Volga steppe. Bow-topped carts continued to play a prominent role for several centuries after the Mongol era, though by the twentieth century their use was limited to just one tribe.

The white cart tent in the foreground of the painting has been unloaded from its two-wheeled cart and placed on the ground next to the darker collapsible yurt. Note the more pointed profile of the portable yurt and the flatter silhouette of the cart tent.

force in the development of Tibetan Buddhism. The evolution of the yurt diverged with these two distinct tribal streams.

THE TURKIC ÜY

The yurt among the Turkic tribes retains much of its form from the time of Chingiz Khan. Variations developed between Turkic tribal groups due to factors such as climate, culture, economic developments, and the kinds of transport animals available (for example, camels versus horses or yak).[21] However, the basic structure of the Turkic yurt is the same throughout Central Asia, and it remains distinct from the Mongolian version.

The Turkic tribes call their round nomadic

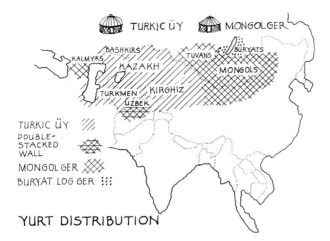

TURKIC ÜY   MONGOL GER

TURKIC ÜY ///
DOUBLE-
STACKED
WALL
MONGOL GER
BURYAT LOG GER :::

YURT DISTRIBUTION

This map shows the locations of the two basic versions of yurts,
Turkic and Mongol, and their distribution across tribal lines. Also
shown are the locations of the Afghan yurts, which employ a double-
stocked wall, and the Siberian log ger.

shelters *üy* (pronounced "uiy" or "ooee"), *öy, ev,* or
ög. In Turkic dialects, these terms mean simply
"home" or "dwelling."[22]

The Turkic tribes distinguish between *qara üy* or
"black dwelling" (the ordinary yurt) and *aq üy* or
"white dwelling." The lighter colored ("white") felt
is made with less-common white wool and is therefore considered more desirable, being reserved for
weddings and ceremonial purposes or afforded
only by the wealthy.[23]

The rounded (many have called it "domed")
shape of the *üy* comes from its bentwood roof
struts. The simple, lightweight center ring is also
carried over from earlier times; however, the
number of slats placed across the ring varies from
tribe to tribe. The trellis walls are usually four or
five feet tall.

The *üy* has a simple, lightweight door frame that
is taken apart for transport. Usually the threshold is
low, although it may be taller in snowy climates.

The door, until recently, was still made from felt,
often backed with a reed screen for stiffness. Only
in the last few generations have most of the tribes
begun using double wooden doors, sometimes in
addition to the felt flap (formerly wooden doors
were used by tribal leaders only).

The Turkic yurt typically has a felted door flap or double wooden
doors, as in these photographs of Kirghiz yurts. The trefoil appliqué
and the bands crisscrossing the roof felts are also typical of Kirghiz
and Kazakh yurts.

The Turkic yurt, or *üy*, is distinguished by its bentwood roof struts
and simple, lightweight roof wheel. Note also the simple door frame
and the tension band encircling the trellis wall.

Three different woven belts are used with the üy. One belt, which can be thin or wide, stretches from the door frame around the upper perimeter of the üy at the level of the top trellis crossing. This functions as the tension band, holding the trellis wall in place against the outward thrust of the roof struts. A wide bellyband may be tied around the center of the trellis wall. A third thin belt is wound around each roof strut in turn, holding the struts at the correct spacing and keeping them from twisting. The three bands are decorative as well as functional.

Some tribes in Afghanistan share a unique version of the üy with a steeper roof profile and an extended central ring. These yurts sometimes have two trellis walls, one stacked on top of the other, with a wide central waistband holding them in place. This double wall may have developed in situations where camels were not available for transport and other smaller pack animals had to be used. (The normal trellis wall is perfectly sized for transport by tall Bactrian camels.)

TOP LEFT: This two-tiered, pointed yurt from northwestern Afghanistan is a possible direct descendent of the yurts of the Mongol era. Note the double curve of the roof struts and the pointed profile of the tall roof wheel.

BOTTOM LEFT: In this Afghan yurt frame, one trellis is stacked on another to create a double-stacked wall. Note also how the roof strut spacing is maintained with a band that winds from strut to strut.

TOP RIGHT: These are typical yurts of the Turkmen tribe, with reed walls and a domed shape. A white wedding yurt (aq üy) is in front; behind is the dark yurt (quara üy) that belongs to the bridegroom's father.

BOTTOM RIGHT: Inside the wedding yurt, the felts are raised to allow for ventilation through the outer reed wall. Note the plain, white tension band near the top of the trellis wall.

    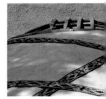

Kirghiz yurts are known for their color and decoration. The photo on the far left shows a framework painted a bright red color and roof struts attached to the trellis wall using the typical Turkic figure-eight pattern. The second photo shows a brightly patterned reed wall with a felted appliqué band above it. The women in the center photo are appliquéing a similar band. The last two photos show brightly colored tassels hung from the roof wheel and decorative bands used for securing the wall and roof felts.

View toward the place of honor in a highly decorated Kazakh yurt. Woven bands, which attach the wall felts, crisscross the roof, and a reed screen is used for the inner wall behind the trellis.

Many tribes use reed or cane mats on their walls, often as a summer covering to allow for airflow while keeping out herd animals. They are also used in conjunction with wall felts; sometimes the reed mats are on the outside, sometimes on the inside. The many variations between clans are due the availability of resources, cultural traditions, and climate.

Kirghiz yurts are known for their craftsmanship. Although the yurts are not unusual structurally, the Kirghiz employ more decoration in their yurts than most tribes. Woodwork may be painted red or brown. Colorful interior decoration is supplied by woven reed mats placed between the trellis wall and exterior felts, and reed screens may serve as partitions for the kitchen storage area. A typical Kirghiz yurt is full of multihued rugs and woven elements, with brightly colored decorative tassels hanging from the roof ring.

The Kazakhs, too, often add decoration to their yurts. Both Kazakh and Kirghiz families sometimes decorate their exterior roof and wall felts with appliqué work around the lower edge; trefoil motifs are typical. The door felt also may be appliquéd or embroidered with designs.[24]

There are also regional, tribal, and sometimes

seasonal differences between groups. For example, tribal groups may be known for their use of a particular shade of felt, determined by the kind of sheep they have, what they can afford, and their method of making felt. Although white is generally preferred (see aq üy on page 22), there are tribes known for using brown or gray. Unique patterns are often used when crisscrossing the roof to tie down the outer felts; these patterns help to distinguish one clan from its neighbors. A seasonal difference occurs when one clan makes the circumference of their yurts smaller in the winter, giving themselves a steeper roofline to facilitate rain runoff.

Although yurts are the most common shelter used by Turkic pastoralists, other tent types are also widespread. These include benders, rib tents, and strut or armature tents (also known as *alachig*, which are more dome shaped than the Turkic üy and have no trellis wall).

The *alachig* is used by Turkic nomads. The shelter is reminiscent of the roof struts of the Turkic yurt with the trellis wall removed. The felts in this picture are raised for ventilation, revealing reed skirting that provides privacy and keeps herd animals out.

THE MONGOLIAN GER

Mongolians call their shelter *ger* (rhymes with "air" or "ear"). Like the Turkic term *üy*, the Mongolian word *ger* also simply means "home" or "dwelling." It is sacred space as well as home space, providing in its very structure a daily visualization of tribal cosmology for all members of the household.

The modern ger has gone through numerous structural changes from the time of Chingiz Khan, but it exhibits less modulation between tribes than does its Turkic cousin. The straight roof struts of the ger are reminiscent of the tipi of the Siberian Buryat people, who claim their land as the birthplace of the Mongol tribes. The profile of the portable ger also resembles the Buryat wooden ger, an eight-sided log building that may well predate the portable ger as a tribal dwelling.[25]

The profile of the ger roof, lower than its Turkic counterparts, has the advantage of leaving the ger less susceptible to the fierce winds and dangerous lightening storms of the steppes. The central ring, or crown, is a heavy mortise-and-tenoned wheel. Some think the design of eight spokes within the ring developed as an expression of the Buddhist eight-fold path. The ring is raised with two decorated supports, which are usually left in place. On a very large ger, the crown may have ten spokes and require four or more support columns.

A "wind rope" hangs from the roof wheel and is looped back into the roof struts until needed during bad weather. The rope is then brought down and either pegged to the ground or weighted with a large stone or a sack of stones for added wind resistance.

The wooden framework of the ger is usually painted bright red with intricate designs. The heavy wooden door is considered a symbol of status and

Palatial reception yurt at Gandan Monastery in Ulan Bator, capital of Mongolia. Four supports with braces are used to help hold up the center ring, and an inside covering hangs over the trellis wall. Note the altar set up to the north (left side of photo).

The Mongolian yurt, called a *ger*, uses straight roof struts that meet at the center in a heavy roof wheel with eight spokes. The ger has a solid door frame and a crafted wooden door. Three simple bands encircle the ger to hold the felts in place.

is usually painted in bright colors and then decorated. The heavy door frame includes a high threshold piece built into the bottom of the doorway to keep out snow in the winter and herd animals in the summer. Sometimes a felt flap is added in front of the door and decorated with stitching or appliqué.

The Mongolians use felts to cover their ger and typically do not decorate them.[26] It takes a minimum of seven felts to make a complete set: four rectangular or trapezoidal felts for the walls, two semicircular felts for the roof, and a diamond-shaped smoke-hole cover. Old felts that are worn or smoke damaged are added in the winter for multiple layers of insulation.

The heavy wooden door of a Mongolian ger is considered a symbol of status. Doors are usually painted in bright colors and are often highly decorated.

Over the felts, modern families often add a canvas or cotton outer covering to help repel water and keep the ger looking white. Many also use an inner liner under the felts to brighten the interior and protect the felts from smoke damage. The inner and outer covering are usually factory produced.

While Turkic tribes are renowned for their weaving skills, the Mongolians rarely weave. Instead, they use ropes made from animal hair (primarily horsehair but also camel and goat). A double braided rope functions as the tension band around the top of the trellis wall, and two or three rope bands secure the wall felts on the outside. In the summer, the bottom of the wall felt may be raised and tucked up under one of the ropes for added ventilation. The smoke hole is opened and closed, using a long rope attached to the felt cover, to create drafts when desired, adjust for wind direction, and provide protection. The top felt is closed at night.

Like the Turkic tribes, the Mongols have other forms of traditional shelter in addition to the portable ger. The Buryat tribes that live in northern Mongolia and in Siberia see their eight-sided log ger as simply more permanent versions of the portable lattice-walled shelters. Families may use the log ger in the winter and switch to the portable ger when they head for better grazing areas in the summer. The Buryat also use two versions of the tipi: a portable tipi covered with caribou hides and a more permanent structure covered in bark.

This painting is taken from the film *Mujaan*, which features a nomadic family that specializes in ger making. The basic steps of making a yurt are shown: in the lower left, sheep are sheared, the wool is beaten to clean it and fluff it up, and then it is layered and rolled around a log to be dragged across the steppe by horse or camel until it becomes felt. Above that, a skilled carpenter cuts down a tree from which he makes roof struts, the roof wheel, door, and lattice walls. Finally, the finished ger is put up (top left), covered in felt, and a feast of celebration is prepared (top right). The two-wheeled cart for transporting the ger is shown being made in the middle.

CRAFTING THE YURT

"The material [to make a yurt] is almost always of local provenance, wool or hair from the herds, leather, and the timber to hand: its use arises directly from the techniques available, without affectation. Compared to our own extravagance, this is exemplary."

–Peter Alford Andrews,
TENT TYPES OF THE MIDDLE EAST

All the materials of the Central Asian yurt are available on the steppe and can be processed by the herders themselves. However, it is common practice for nomads to purchase the wooden framework from a nomad carpenter or a settled craftsman who lives near a source of wood (usually willow or fir) and has the requisite tools and equipment on hand. The Mongolian roof wheel and door, in particular, require carpentry tools and skills.[27]

The structural framework of the yurt consists of four parts:

o— wall frame (in four or more lattice sections)
o— door frame (with or without a wooden door)
o— roof wheel or crown
o— set of roof struts

Lattice wall construction is the same for Mongol and Turkic yurts. Each wall unit is made up of ten to sixteen whole willow rods (or split wooden laths) that run in each direction; shorter rods make up the corners. Holes are drilled in the rods at a precise (but nonuniform) spacing with either a hot iron or a bow drill. Then wet rawhide strips are knotted, pulled through the hole, knotted again, and cut. As the hide dries, it tightens and draws the slats together.

The crisscrosses at the top of the wall are called

"heads," and at the bottom they are called "feet." Usually the foot sections are longer than the head sections to provide greater traction and stability for the yurt and to allow for wear or breakage over time.

A typical yurt uses four lattice wall sections. The Mongols often use five. Wealthy families may have a large yurt of six to eight sections. Palatial yurts, used by religious dignitaries or government officials, may run as large as ten units. Yurt size is also measured by the number of heads along the top of the trellis (corresponding to the number of roof struts). A yurt of sixty head is the standard family size; a yurt of eighty to one hundred head is considered large.

The bentwood roof poles for the Turkic yurt are shaped by soaking and heating them to soften the wood and then bending them in a jig. (This process is also used with the lath pieces, which are given a slight bend, and the two halves of the Turkic roof wheel.) In a nomadic situation, the poles are heated in a pile of composting dung, or a flue is dug into the ground to create a fire or steam box. A barrel stove may be used for the same purpose in a village context.

The jig for the roof poles can be made of pegs

hammered into a log, or it may be a permanent setup. Once bent, the roof poles are stacked and left for up to a week on a template of stakes driven into the ground to set the curve.

Both Turkic and Mongolian roof poles have a hole drilled in the bottom end through which a loop or lanyard is tied. The loop, used on the Mongol ger, is simply slid over the trellis head member. A lanyard, or chord, is used by the Turkic tribes to tie the roof struts to the top of the lattice wall using a figure-eight pattern. The top end of the roof pole, where it is inserted into the center ring, is usually squared to keep the center ring from twisting in high winds. On Turkic yurts the tops of the roof poles may be left rounded and the struts tied with bands at the curve to keep them from twisting.

To make the Turkic crown or center ring, two or three split saplings are bent into semicircles and fastened with rawhide strips or metal hoops. Center

(CLOCKWISE FROM TOP LEFT) A barrel stove is used to heat yurt parts for bending in this Kirghiz village known for its yurt making. A roof pole is placed in the barrel stove steamer to ready it for bending; note the jig standing close by in the background. Then the roof pole is bent on the jig and stacked on a template until the curve is set. The final photo shows drawknives used by the Kirghiz yurt maker.

A Mongol herder finishes a roof strut with a drawknife.

(*CLOCKWISE FROM TOP LEFT*) A flue dug into the ground creates a steam box for a Turkmen yurt builder. The fire is built in front using dung for fuel. Behind, the flue stakes have been driven into the ground to create templates where the finished pieces are stacked for up to a week until the required curve is set. The photo on the top right shows the yurt builder using a jig to bend a pole that has been softened in the steam box into the rim of a roof wheel. The image on the bottom shows a Mongolian craftsman burning squared holes in a new center ring using a red hot iron.

cross pieces made from willow rods are placed in precut holes on the inside of the ring. The holes are angled so that the cross pieces arch slightly above the ring. Square or round holes are made around the perimeter of the ring to receive the roof poles.

The roof poles may be slightly charred or painted with certain pigments to protect them from bug infestations. A yurt frame should last up to fifty years, or one generation.

creating the felts

Legend has it that felt was invented—or rather discovered—by Central Asian horse riders who placed wool under their saddles to protect their horses' backs from abrasion. The combination of moisture and warmth from the horse and the constant agitation of riding turned the wool into felt.[28]

Wool fibers have tiny epidermal scales (as many as two thousand scales per inch of fiber) that overlap in one direction along a single hair, like fish scales or the scales on a pinecone. When agitated, the fibers get tangled as they bend around each other. The scales keep the fibers from backing out, thereby creating a mat of tangled fibers that becomes felt.

Sprinkling warm water on the fibers causes the scales to push outward and catch more easily. Adding soap also promotes swelling of the fibers and opening of the scales. Uncleaned wool requires less soap as it retains more of its natural fats and salts. (Wool can be felted without soap, but the process takes longer.) Increasing the temperature of the water speeds up the felting process. The ideal felting temperature is between 104 and 122 degrees Fahrenheit, although the water used by the nomads is not this hot.

Wool has many properties that make it perfect as a shelter covering. A great insulator against both heat and cold, wool is naturally flame resistant (when on fire, it smolders without giving off heat). When tightly crimped, as it is in felt, the material absorbs odors and noise. The felting process not only makes wool warmer, it also makes it less permeable and more water resistant.

The seven felts of a typical yurt require from sixty to as many as one hundred and ninety wool fleeces, depending on the size of the yurt, the desired thickness of the felt, and the type of wool being used.[29]

The methods for felting vary, depending on whether a nomadic family is felting using pack animals and resources at hand to meet its own needs, or whether local craftspeople in a village are producing and selling felted yurt covers to the nomadic population. In the village context, different methods are used to increase production, and machines or people perform the work that pack animals perform on the steppe. Other variations in felting procedures have to do with the availability of reed mats for use in the process and the decorative touches that tribal groups add.

Techniques used by the steppe nomads are the most basic. Felt is made in the fall, usually around the end of August or beginning of September, using the wool from the second shearing of the sheep (the first is in the spring).[30] All members of the household participate; a master felter (usually a woman) is in charge.[31]

Feltmaking is an all-day process that begins with a toast of fermented mares' milk and ends with a feast of roast lamb. The opening ceremony and post-felting party are considered essential elements of the process.

Before feltmaking begins, the wool is placed in a pile and beaten with willow or iron rod to clean the wool and fluff it up.

In Mongolia, an old felt, called the "mother felt," is blessed by the feltmaker and rolled out. The best and whitest wool is laid out by hand on this mother

Before wool is used for felting, it is beaten with rods to fluff it up. This also helps to clean the wool.

The first layer of wool is carefully laid out on the mother felt. This first layer is usually the whitest and cleanest wool. The second layer, which will not be seen from either side, can be rougher and darker. Sometimes whole fleeces are used in this center layer.

felt. This will become the "good" side or outside of the felt. Unwashed and unbeaten fleeces may be used in the middle layer. The final layer is coarser, darker wool that has been beaten. This will become the back side of the felt.

Some feltmakers sprinkle each layer of wool with water before adding the next layer. Others wait until the layering of the wool is complete before sprinkling the entire felt with water. Sometimes the water is heated; in other instances it is not.

Next, a large pole is placed at one end, and the

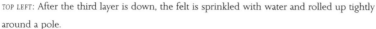

TOP LEFT: After the third layer is down, the felt is sprinkled with water and rolled up tightly around a pole.

TOP RIGHT: The felt roll is wrapped in animal skins, in this case a horse hide, and tied with ropes. Lines are attached to the pole so that the felt can be pulled behind an animal.

BOTTOM RIGHT: A felt is pulled behind a camel in western Mongolia.

mother felt and new wool are rolled tightly around the pole. Wet hides are wrapped around the felt roll and tied with strong rope or leather straps. More water may be added at this point. Then a long rope is attached to the pole at both ends and the entire roll is dragged across the steppe by either horses or a camel.

After a number of hours, the roll is unwrapped and examined. Weak spots are strengthened with wool or horsehair, the felt is sprinkled with water, and then the mother felt and wool are rolled up again. The process may be repeated a few times before the new felt is separated from the mother felt. The Mongols ritually proclaim that "a sweet daughter has been born" and then they may add more layers of wool to the daughter felt to get the desired thickness, repeating the felting process once again.

When the feltmaker is satisfied with the new felt, it is set aside to dry. Several felts can be made in one day. When the felting is complete, the party begins.

In the village, a reed mat is usually placed beneath the felt. A mother felt may or may not be used. Any designs are carefully laid out, using a small three-pronged comb, called a *cubuk*. The whitest wool is placed over the designs and the rest of the wool is layered over that. The entire assemblage is rolled up, tied tightly, and then rolled back and forth. A felting machine may be used, the roll may be kicked back and forth between two or more people, or a rope can be looped around the felt and used to roll it back and forth. The roll is periodically opened to check its progress, weak spots are addressed, and more wool is added, if necessary.

New felts look fresh and clean, but the brand-new look doesn't last long, as felt readily picks up dust and grime. Smoke inside the yurt gradually

(*LEFT TO RIGHT*) Kirghiz felt makers begin by spreading out the first layer of wool for a yurt wall panel. In the second photo, a darker layer of felt is added, followed by a third layer. Hot, soapy water is poured over the felt as the panel is rolled up in grass matting and canvas and then tied securely. The felt is then rolled for an hour on this simple felting machine, after which the finished felt panel is set aside to dry.

turns the felts first brown and then black. Initially this makes the felt more waterproof, but by the time a felt turns black (after about ten years) it becomes too brittle to fold for travel.

As the felts darken, they may be used for separate kitchen yurts (where the cooking takes place in the summer) or placed between other felts for extra insulation in the winter. Eventually they become saddle blankets or are turned to other uses. Contemporary yurt dwellers stretch the life of their felts by using a factory-produced canvas covering for protection on the outside, and a cotton layer inside the felt. This provides additional rain protection and keeps the yurt looking fresh much longer.

TRAVELING WITH THE YURT

Pastoral nomads traditionally move through four seasonal encampments (winter, spring, summer, and fall), though the time spent in each varies from a few weeks to many months. Some groups only migrate between summer and winter camps. The longest encampment is winter, usually from November to April. Many nomads return to the same winter camp every year and may build permanent sheds and corrals or a short rock wall to encircle the yurt.

This yurt design is ideal for transporting on two, or possibly three, Bactrian camels. The frame is loaded onto one camel with equal loads on each side. The roof wheel is loaded last; it fits neatly over the hump. The felts are loaded onto a second camel. Where camels are not available, the herders use yak or horses to haul yurts on carts, or the yurts may be driven to their new destination in a Russian truck. As was noted earlier, the double-trellis design found in Afghanistan was probably developed for use with smaller pack animals.

Two or three Bactrian camels can comfortably carry a medium-sized yurt and household goods.

SETTING UP THE YURT

Because the steppes of Central Asia are very dry, nomads set up their yurts directly on the grassy plain, placing rugs and felted mats over the ground inside. In winter, felts are layered wall to wall as protection from the permafrost below. Outside the yurt, a narrow "skirting" felt encircles the bottom of the yurt. Dirt is piled against the yurt or over the bottom of the skirting felt, providing an airtight seal against windblown snow. What little precipitation does occur is usually in the form of snow, so there is little danger of water leaking or flooding inside the yurt. Snow can easily be beaten off the roof.

In cities like Ulan Bator, where as many as fifty thousand people live in yurts at the outskirts of the city, pallets or wood decking are used to create a floor. The yurt is set up on the wooden deck, and felted mats and rugs are layered on the deck for insulation and warmth.

Usually three to five people work together to set up a yurt, which takes about thirty minutes to an hour. First, they stretch out the lattice sections and tie them together to form a circle, which includes the door frame. Then either the top (tension) band or a middle bellyband is brought around the perimeter and attached to the door frame.

Many Mongolians live in ger in cities or towns for all or part of the year. Town ger are typically in a fenced area and may be surrounded by a number of small outbuildings. In the winter, a skirting felt is placed around the bottom of the yurt. Dirt has been piled over the skirting felt on this ger, creating an airtight seal against cold air and windblown snow.

The Mongols tie or dowel two center ring supports to the center ring. The ring is raised using the center ring supports, and then the roof poles are placed in the ring and attached with a loop (or bridle) to the top of the lattice wall.

The Turkic center ring is raised using three or four roof struts at equidistant spacing that are then tied off to the lattice wall heads using a chord or lanyard in a figure eight. (Often someone helps to balance the center ring using a stick or special tool.) Then the rest of the struts are placed.

If an inner lining is used, it goes up next, and then the wall and roof felts. The order in which the felts go up varies. On the Turkic üy, the wall felts may be hung with loops from the top of the lattice wall, or they are attached with decorative bands that cross over the roof struts to the trellis heads on the opposite side of the yurt. The Mongolians tie the wall felts off with two or three side ropes. The roof felts are pulled up and tied, and finally the smoke-hole cover is pulled over the smoke hole and adjusted for wind and weather needs.

(TOP TO BOTTOM) In this photo sequence, a family of Turkmen nomads erects their yurt. First the trellis sections adjacent to the door frame are expanded and attached to the door frame. Then the rest of the trellis sections are expanded and attached. A wide bellyband is attached to the door frame and encircles the trellis wall, holding everything in place. In the top middle photo, the roof wheel is raised using four sets of struts, with one person helping in the middle. In the bottom middle photo, the rest of the struts are placed and wound with a band to maintain their spacing and keep them from twisting. In the bottom photo, an additional tension band is brought around the yurt at the junction where trellis wall and roof struts meet.

LIFE WITHIN THE GER: THE SACRED CIRCLE

For Mongolians (and some Turkic tribes), the ger is more than their traveling shelter on the Asian steppes. It is their cosmological centering point in a moving universe.

The threshold, a tall step or sill tied into the door frame of the ger, has always been held sacred. Touching or stepping on the threshold when entering is considered an extreme insult to the owner of the ger. The threshold represents not only the distinction between the life of the family and the outside world, its importance also reinforces the idea of the dwelling itself as sacred.[32]

The internal floor plan of the ger is based on the four directions, much like the Native American medicine wheel. The door of the ger always opens to the south. Opposite the door, the north is the sacred space and place of perspective. If the family is Buddhist, an altar sits in the north, and it is the place of honor for guests (since it faces the doorway and the sun). The spokes of the roof wheel are aligned with the directions as is the square hearth below in which the fire burns.

Directions in the ger are given as if one were seated in the north, facing south towards the door. For example, an object located in the southwest corner of the ger would be said to exist "to the right of the door." The names for the four directions also correspond to this perspective: south is "front," north is "back," east and west are "left" and "right" respectively.

Masculine and feminine (the Buddhist yin and yang) hold space to the west and east. The western half of the ger is the male area and the eastern half is the female domain. Men's possessions (like riding

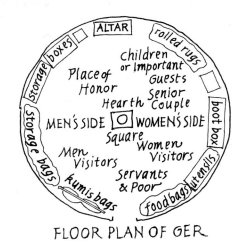

FLOOR PLAN OF GER

The internal floor plan of the Mongolian ger is based on the four directions. The door always opens to the south, and the north is the place of sacred space. The western half of the yurt is the men's side, and the eastern half is the women's area. The fire is the sacred center, and one moves around the yurt in a clockwise direction.

tack and hunting gear) are hung on the western wall sections, and men usually sit to the west. Women's tools (such as pots and pans and felting equipment) are stored on the east side of the ger, where women and children sit.

One proceeds around the ger in a clockwise direction, following the path of the sun (the nomad's clock) as it enters the smoke hole and rotates around the ger through the day. The "sun-wise" direction is also followed in shamanic dances and rituals both inside and outside of the ger.

The fire is seen as the sacred center and the gateway from the middle world (inside the ger) to the world below. The smoke hole above the fire is the entryway to the world above. The smoke rising from the central fire represents the World Tree, which the haman ascends to get to the world above.[33]

In the shamanist tradition, it is the ger itself that holds yin and yang and the worlds above and below in balance. All is centered around the sacred fire, provider of warmth and light and the smoke that rises to the world above. In this way, the ger expresses the unity and balance of all things in the one, the circle.[34]

There are many parallels between the Mongol tribes, in particular the Buryat of Siberia, and Native American traditions, especially those of the Navajo. The eight-sided Navajo hogan, which resembles the Buryat log ger, maintains a strikingly similar internal structure to that of the ger, except that the door faces east and all the directions are adjusted accordingly. (Interestingly, the Mongol ger originally faced east, changing to the south around the thirteenth century, due perhaps to Chinese influence.[35]) Male and female halves in the hogan are to the left and right of the door, sacred space is opposite the door, and all movement flows in a clockwise or sunwise direction (as it also does in the sacred sweat lodge and in Native American dances).

The four directions are of primary importance in both cultures. Willem van Rubruck records the Mongol associations in Chingiz Khan's era of east with air, south with fire, west with water, and north with the dead.[36]

What is perhaps most strikingly different from modern Western models is the Mongolian (and Navajo) concept of home as sacred space. Mongolian and Navajo cosmology isn't taught in a university or exhibited in a cathedral. It is woven into the very fabric of the home space, which in turn conveys to these indigenous tribes an intimate knowledge of their place in the universe, constantly bringing them back from their wandering to the center so that they can live *tegsh*, in balance with the world.[37]

THE GIFT OF THE NOMAD

"We have much to learn from the nomads about living. Our society is highly mobile, but we have adopted few of the tools that make nomadic life a pleasure. Even if we never live in a tent, there is much to be said for the nomad's way of life under the tent roof."

—Torvald Faegre,
TENTS: *ARCHITECTURE OF THE NOMADS*

The Buryat tribes of Siberia see their eight-sided log ger as a permanent version of the portable yurt. This ger strongly resembles the feminine version of the North American Navajo hogan and employs a similar internal ordering as well.

ИРКУТСК
Музей деревянного зодчества "Тальцы"

Юрта западных бурят. XIX в.

If we are open to it, the yurt may be able to teach us who we are and take us back to our mystical source. The image of smoke rising from the fire at the center of the ger can take us beyond ourselves, and this middle world we live in, to connect us to the earth beneath our feet and the sky god above—both at the same time and never one without the other. The ger's fire sits at the center between masculine and feminine, a wheel eternally spinning both energies into balance—and, again, never one without the other. And, finally, there is the daily arc of the sun circling the four directions inside the ger, directions that connect us to the circle of seasons and the cycles of life. Going out from the yurt, we can carry this knowledge of where we stand, between earth and heaven and yin and yang, always connected to the seasons and cycles of life through the four directions.

With this knowledge, it becomes possible for us to take in other gifts. The Central Asian nomads live with deep-rooted simplicity. Nomads carry with them what they need. Each person, for example, brings his or her own cup, bowl, and utensils when travelling. Waste is unthinkable; once something has served its usefulness in one area, it is put to use as something else. Every possession is chosen with care and ideally serves multiple functions. With few possessions, there is the opportunity to bring artistry to every element of daily life. And because everything has its place in the circle of nomadic life (a placement prescribed by the very fabric of the culture), the setting of daily life is greatly simplified. One can walk into any ger and know where most items are stored and what part of the ger is used for which functions. This level of simplicity liberates energy for art, laughter, family, and tribe.

A final gift of the nomads is their intimate sense of connectedness. The circle is the symbol of interconnectedness, and the yurt makes this very real by creating a space for the family to live together in one large room, all the generations, interacting and creating a sense of tribe and family. Likewise, the veil between inside and outside is much thinner in a yurt; one knows when the wind blows or the temperature drops. The earth is truly underfoot, the night sky is visible through the smoke hole, and a sheep bleating in the middle of the night wakes up the herder. It is from this intimate sense of connection with all things around them that nomads talk about living in balance in such a way that Mother Earth is never harmed.

"If in our lifetime we suppress nomads, we shall have done by human harshness what natural harshness could not do. To abolish nomads because they have other skills, know other things, hold other aspirations, and live by other customs than ours—in short, because they are different—is as unwise as it is unworthy. . . . There is a place for nomads in the world, often enough a place we cannot use without them. We must not steal it from them, for if we do, we reduce the richness of human life—we rob ourselves."

—Neville Dyson-Hudson, NOMADS OF THE WORLD

THE TAPERED WALL YURT

"Anyone who has explored the world of folk shelter has had to face this question: why are so many indigenous homes so lovely and modern ones so cold, harsh, and rigid? . . . I am not asking for copies—we are a different people living in a different time. Reproductions are not the answer. Yet can we not capture the spirit of folk designs and build homes that fit our own times and materials as beautifully as our ancestors did? I think that we can, if enough people will take part in the search."

—Bill Coperthwaite, *A Handmade Life*

Imagine a hobbit with a Harvard doctorate who lives on the rocky coastal shoreline of a rich and powerful nation. To visit his realm, you must park your car and walk for a mile and a half down a golden sawdust path through dappled sunlight. You cross a beaver pond and pass hawk nests, gradually leaving behind civilization with all its trappings. The forested pathway wanders and winds gently up and down, back and forth, past mushrooms and ferns, eventually opening up to wildflowers and lowbush blueberries.

Those who make the pilgrimage to Dickinson's Reach (named for poet Emily Dickinson) find a land outside of modern technology's grasp. Here there are no phones, television, or computers; there are no traffic sounds. This is a working homestead, but without chainsaws cutting firewood or tractors molding earth. Not even the background hum of a refrigerator disturbs the silence, which is deep and still. One

Dickinson's Reach in the northeast corner of Maine is the home of Bill Coperthwaite, designer of the tapered wall yurt. The yurts on Bill's property have outwardly slanting walls and are made of cedar. The multitiered yurt in the bottom photo is Bill's home and the repository of the library and archives of the Yurt Foundation.

To get to Dickinson's Reach, the visitor must hike a mile and a half down a golden sawdust path through the forest, gradually moving away from the hustle and bustle of the world and the reach of modern technology.

Approaching the multitiered home of the Yurt Foundation from the forest, one passes an elevated food storage yurt. Even the outbuildings at Dickinson's Reach are small and magical versions of the tapered wall yurt.

hears only birdsong and human conversation, the sound of an axe falling on firewood, and crooked knives hollowing out wooden spoons and bowls.

Bill Coperthwaite lives on this gentle, forested land, held in the embrace of the sea, in a house that resembles a multitiered mushroom or some extraordinary intergalactic wooden spaceship from a universe far away.

In addition to his professional path of educator, Bill is also designer, philosopher, anthropologist, community builder, backwoodsman, and imagineer. He lives and teaches simplicity as a radical reinvention of life. By example, he challenges each observer to pause in the rush for material gain, listen for a moment to the natural world, and learn from indigenous people–from both their crafts and technologies and their practice of carving out a life in harmony with the natural world.

The woodland trail ends at Bill's back door, just past an elevated food storage yurt and tiny outhouse yurt. The bottom floor of Bill's yurt holds five years worth of firewood, neatly stacked. Bill cuts the wood with an axe and bow saw nearly every day; this way the task is never arduous and he keeps his pile continually stocked.

Crossing the yurt, one steps up into a workshop that smells of earth and wood shavings. Hand tools are within reach and neatly organized. Work stools, a hammock, and a glassed-in reading nook complete the picture of a shop dedicated to handwork and enveloped in comfort and warmth.

Stairs lead up to a second floor that is completely encircled with windows, displaying a panoramic view of the world. Living spaces are delineated by the furniture they contain. Curvaceous shelves filled with wooden bowls and mugs define the kitchen

A little outhouse yurt can be seen just in front of the Yurt Foundation Archives and Library Yurt. The bottom floor of the multitiered yurt provides firewood storage and encloses Bill Coperthwaite's workshop area. The second floor is divided between Bill's living space and the archives of the Yurt Foundation. The top floor is a bedroom surrounded by windows and topped with a cupola.

area; on the floor sits a wooden bucket filled with drinking water. Across from the kitchen in the center of the yurt (and tucked behind a ladder leading up to the top floor) is the pantry and food-storage area. A sitting room with couches and chairs stretches beyond the pantry; this is a place where friends gather in the evening for reading, conversation, and storytelling. Farthest from the entry is a study area with a desk built into the slanting wall and shelves full of books. Here Bill spends part of his day writing articles and books and responding to letters from around the world.

Meals and meetings happen in the sitting room, the social heart of the Yurt Foundation, where Bill Coperthwaite's friends gather to discuss issues, share a meal, and tell stories. In the background, note Bill's writing desk and, to the left of that, the Yurt Foundation Archives.

Children love to climb up into the cupola and see the view from the topmost tier of the big yurt.

The rest of the main floor contains the library and archives of the Yurt Foundation. There are volumes on indigenous people and their technologies. A little exploration turns up books on hand tools, blacksmithing, and wood carving. Articles are filed in drawers under the seating and in built-in wall cabinets. Baskets hold treasures of native crafts collected from around the world, and a quick glance takes in photographs of yurts, kayaks, and Eskimo fishing lures.

Between the archives and the pantry area is a ladder leading to the top floor. This is Bill's bedroom with slanted walls and a circle of windows. It is a smaller version of the main floor. At the center of the roof is an open compression ring topped with a cupola, the fourth and final tier of this "wedding cake" house.

From the multitiered Library Yurt, guests can meander down a trail towards the Mill Pond inlet and the sea. Just off the trail and hidden in the woods is the little Study Yurt, with a surround of windows and a built-in semicircular desk. The fortunate occupant can work protected from the elements while completely enveloped in the forest green of the surroundings.

Bill Coperthwaite's small Study Yurt is hidden from passersby. It is just large enough for one person to sit in, surrounded on three sides by a built-in desk.

Continuing down the trail one arrives at the Guest Yurt, a twenty-eight-foot concentric yurt. (A concentric yurt consists of one muffin-shaped yurt tucked inside another; the two yurts share the same roof. The smaller inner yurt is elevated, providing ample storage space beneath.) A wide ledge resting on the outer wall of the Guest Yurt creates an extended bed that circles two-thirds of the structure. Under the hinged ledge are blankets and guest supplies. There is plenty of room, and those who hike in and stay overnight are well cared for here.

Beyond the Guest Yurt is the peaceful Mill Pond

Down the hill from the multitiered yurt is the Guest Yurt, a light-filled concentric yurt with an elevated inner yurt that provides extra storage and floor space. A ledge resting on the inner wall of the yurt makes a long bed that circles two-thirds of the structure and provides storage underneath for guest supplies like blankets, sweaters, and extra shoes for clamming.

inlet, frequented by herons and waterfowl of all sorts. This is also the center of the human social scene. Many summer guests arrive by water. Some row in from sailboats, but most put in their boats at an inlet a couple of miles away and canoe or kayak over. They are greeted by the mushroom-shaped Kitchen Yurt, only twelve feet in diameter but able to squeeze in eight guests around a table in stormy weather. Those arriving in sunny weather are welcomed to an outdoor circle of log rounds nearby, spaced around a large table.

With his ruddy complexion and halo of white hair, Bill looks far younger than his seventy-plus years. His piercing blue eyes spark fire when he discusses simple living and social design, issues of

The mushroom-like Kitchen Yurt greets guests arriving by water and creates a centering point for social gatherings on the Mill Pond Inlet. The original birch bark roof, seen here, was later replaced with cedar shingles.

Workshops and classes are held at Dickinson's Reach, and guests either hike in or arrive by water at the Mill Pond inlet to take classes or spend time with Bill Coperthwaite (pictured above).

overpopulation, or a capitalist system out of control. Most of the time, though, conversation with friends and guests revolves around what family members are doing or how neighbors feel about encroaching development along the Maine shoreline.

For some guests, the visit to Dickinson's Reach is an annual pilgrimage. With family in tow, they come to see this peaceful kingdom and draw from the inspiration of its magical buildings. Children shriek with delight as their parents push them in a rope swing, and parents remember the summer when they, too, were seven and soaring ever higher on the same swing. Some visitors share a picnic lunch with Bill; others merely shake hands and continue hiking through the giant trees along the shoreline.

THE YURT FOUNDATION

"Imagine what would happen if three hundred million people were concerned with building a better world! This would be a social revolution such as has never been conceived. The key difference would be people coming to the realization that it is their world: that it can be changed, that they can, should, and must have a role in redesigning that world."

–Bill Coperthwaite, A HANDMADE LIFE

Bill Coperthwaite believes that design belongs to the people and that everyone, including children, should have a hand in creating their lives and the objects that surround them. As a high school teacher and Harvard doctoral student, Bill was inspired by the potential of the Mongolian yurt as the basis for a sustainable shelter design that people could build themselves.

Bill Coperthwaite calls his place and his work the Yurt Foundation, which is fitting. It is because of Bill that yurts migrated to the West.

Long before he came to live on his Maine homestead full-time, Bill was an educator, an unusual one who believed that the best teacher is also a learner and that instilling an excitement for living and for constant exploration is more important than communicating facts. Many of Bill's students were inspired and deeply affected by their contact with him.

In 1962, while teaching at a Quaker school in New Hampshire, Bill saw an article in *National Geographic* with photographs of Mongolian yurts. Bill was fascinated by the nomadic yurts and inspired by the idea of the yurt as an indigenous design that could be adapted to create accessible, livable forms of shelter.

At the time, Bill's senior math class was exploring the mathematics of roof design. For a class project, they took the design of a yurt roof and modified it, replacing the straight rafters with a lattice framework. Together they built a sample roof and confirmed that, indeed, a central compression ring was no longer necessary with the lattice roof. (However, when one of Bill's math students, Chuck Cox, created plans a few years later for the modern fabric yurt, he returned to the original Mongolian design of straight rafters.)

Bill's next teaching assignment was in Grass Valley, California. There his class built a complete yurt with sloped lattice walls, a lattice roof structure, and a cloth covering.

Bill decided that yurts had great potential as a teaching and community-building tool. To test his theory (and as part of his Harvard doctoral program),

This early yurt with a folded-plate (or chevron) roof was built by students at Harvard.

This was the first complete yurt constructed in North America, built in the early 1960s by students in Grass Valley, California. The innovative trellis roof, which requires no center ring, is an example of how Bill Coperthwaite constantly modified the original indigenous design.

The Harvard Yurt was built with boards held in place by a tension band of steel aircraft cable that encircles the upper perimeter of the wall.

he spent the year of 1968 leading a group of high school students in building their own campus, a collection of ten tapered wall yurts. The students were required to write about their experiences and together they created a film about the event. One of those high school students, David Raitt, was so deeply inspired that he went on to build yurts as a profession, eventually developing the design for the frame panel yurt.

To test his theory further, Bill organized a workshop to build a yurt at Harvard University. He then proceeded to hold seminars in the Harvard Yurt, leading discussions with both students and faculty on educational philosophy, sustainable design, and the usefulness of indigenous crafts.

Bill's early yurt-building experiences became the models for ongoing projects with schools and communities. Bill decided to build yurts only in workshops, where everyone could work together and learn from the process. Though his designs continued to evolve with each project, the tapered wall has remained a consistent and defining element.

In 1972, Bill established the Yurt Foundation to continue exploring and sharing his vision of blending wisdom from various cultures, ancient and modern, to invent simpler, more harmonious, and more "democratic" ways of living. For Bill, cultural blending and the thoughtful design of life in every detail (which he calls "social design") are key to maintaining true democracy.

Eventually Bill's search for a "democratic shelter" that was human sized and accessible (something anyone could build with a good set of plans) led him to develop four sets of tapered wall yurt plans to enable people to build their own shelters.

YURT PLANS

The Standard Yurt

The Standard Yurt, which is seventeen feet in diameter at the eaves, is the basic one-room yurt. One of Bill's earliest designs, it can be used as a small seminar room, student living quarters, mountain retreat, or private office.

The Little Yurt

The Little Yurt–ten, twelve, or seventeen feet–is the simplest yurt to build. Plans come with three sets of dimensions. Designed to work in conjunction with the larger yurts, the Little Yurt has uses as diverse as an outhouse and shower unit, small office, child's room, or guesthouse.

The Concentric Yurt

The Concentric Yurt, which is thirty-two feet in diameter at the eaves, is really one yurt inside another. The inner yurt is raised half a story and shares the roof with the outer one, which saves material costs. The resulting under-story space can be used for a couch, bookshelves, or pantry. Concentric yurts are used as permanent homes or summer homes, common rooms in communities, and as seminar and library spaces. They have about five times the room of a standard yurt and are flooded with light from twenty-six encircling windows.

The Family Yurt

The Family Yurt, which is fifty-three feet in diameter at the eaves, is a multitiered yurt that was designed to be built in stages (see diagram below). Bill's goal in designing the Family Yurt was "to provide a structure that would be pleasant to live in while allowing people with little money to build without borrowing." The first stage is a raised concentric yurt, which can be lived in immediately. Then, as more money, time, and energy become available, the family can add an outer ring as the lower floor. Bill followed a similar process in building his multitiered Library and Archives Yurt.

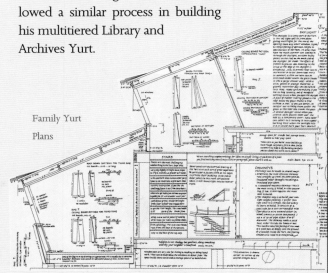

Family Yurt
Plans

Concentric Yurt Floor Layout

Family Yurt Stages

The section of Family Yurt plans above is typical of Bill Coperthwaite's plans, presenting a mixture of drawings, detailed instructions, and words of wit and wisdom. The drawings to the left show the stages in which the Family Yurt can be built. To the far left is a floor layout for the Concentric Yurt, which has a raised inner yurt inside a thirty-two-foot yurt.

Bill suggests slowing down in order to get the most out of the building process:

Take lots of time in building your home. It doesn't have to be completed in six months or a year. Such urgency is a modern ill that has crept upon us unawares. Look at some of the beautiful, old, rambling farm houses of our ancestors; these buildings were often the work of several generations. More relaxed building allows you to come into closer harmony with the structure, to understand it better and to grow in your knowledge of space and design. By giving your skill a longer incubation time, you get a better home.

Much joy has been taken out of home building by hurry. Building its own home can be a great source of joy and companionship for the whole family (there are many parts of this building that small people can take part in), so why not let it take shape over four or five years . . . or a lifetime?

BUILDING A YURT HOME: THE JULIE PRATT STORY

Many people have used Bill's plans to build their own yurts. Julie Pratt bought a set of concentric yurt plans in 1975 after seeing a Yurt Foundation calendar at a store in Berkeley, California. Julie was working at the Berkeley post office and living in the Bay Area with her husband and three children, but she owned property in Washington State and dreamed of living in a rural setting. When she saw the calendar, she knew this was the house she wanted to build.

In 1977, Julie's husband was diagnosed with Lou Gehrig's disease. After he died in 1978, Julie packed up the family's belongings and headed for Tonasket, Washington. Her children were two, six, and eight.

The family stayed at a vacant homestead a half mile from their property during the building process. Julie had already purchased materials from a local mill. The ground was leveled in the spring of 1979 and building began. Neighbors helped with some of the tasks, bringing a generator and cement mixer to help set the twenty-two posts on which the yurt would rest. Other than the cement mixer, only hand tools were used.

It took two weeks to get the basic structure up, minus the roof. Julie and the kids took a break to bring up the last of their possessions from

After her husband died, Julie Pratt and her three children moved to rural Tonasket, Washington, and built this concentric yurt from a set of Bill Coperthwaite's concentric yurt plans. "It was a great learning experience," says Julie. "There's a lot to be said for owners building their own houses; I think it makes for more sound people."

California, and then they moved into the yurt. Fortunately, the weather stayed nice for the next month while they put the roof around their living space and finished the outside siding. "We were ready by winter, except for firewood," says Julie. A couple from the local hardware store came for a visit and cut all of the family's firewood in one day.

Julie was given a trailerload of windows from a Victorian house in San Francisco. "They just fit the openings in the yurt," comments Julie. "They were ideal." Julie made one adjustment to Bill's plans: she left out windows on the north side of the yurt to reduce heat loss during the bitterly cold Tonasket winters.

After the yurt was finished, Julie raised the floor level of the inner yurt by two feet, providing seven feet of headspace underneath, instead of five. "The floor for the upper story hit me right at head level," says Julie. "So we raised it. It was quite an undertaking. We cut out one support at a time with the chainsaw and used logs from the land as our new supports. Those extra two feet of floor height made a huge difference."

Looking back, Julie would have used screws as fasteners instead of nails. "I've learned that screws can take much more stress than nails and will last twice as long," explains Julie. "However, the yurt seems to be doing fine with its nails."

Yurt Living

For the next seven years, Julie and her children lived simply and happily in the yurt. Though temperatures dropped to thirty-five degrees below zero, the family stayed cozy. "We used far less wood in our woodstove than our neighbors because we didn't have all the interior walls portioning off rooms that had to be heated," says Julie. The family carpeted two-thirds of the yurt, adding to the six inches of insulation under the floor, although they never did insulate the ceiling. "I didn't want to cover up its structural beauty or lose the feeling of openness," remarks Julie.

The family used ingenuity to work with the round, slanted walls. Julie designed a combination woodstove, cookstove, and water heater to fit the round walls of the yurt, and a local stove company fabricated it. "In the kitchen," explains Julie, "all your standard appliances stand up vertically, leaving a space behind where the walls lean out, so we found ways that really worked to make use of the space behind. Also, any shelves we built had to be terraced. So we continued building unusual things to make our unusual environment work."

Until Julie brought in a phone line, the family used CB radios to communicate with their neighbors. At night they took turns reading aloud to each other by the light of kerosene and propane lamps, and once a week they gathered around a little battery-powered radio to listen to a mystery radio show. A tub provided hot baths in the winter; in the summer they used an outdoor shower. Well water, a gray-water system, and an outhouse completed their system requirements.

Of the yurt, Julie comments that "it's an amazing thing to have windows all around. You find yourself focused not internally but externally because you are constantly looking out at your surroundings. The wall is leaning away from you, leading your eye out, so you look out the windows and see everything around you, all of your environment. It's an unusual feeling. You can't help but walk around the yurt."

After seven years in their yurt, Julie remarried and the family moved into town. Julie continued to use the skills she acquired by building the yurt, remodeling every house she has subsequently moved into, as well as a restaurant that she ran for ten years.

Julie looks back on her family's yurt-building experience with great fondness. "It was one good learning experience. There's a lot to be said for owners building their own houses; I think it makes for more sound people."

Julie Pratt and her children built their yurt home in one summer. "Building the yurt gave a sense of pride to our family," says Julie. Once the floor and walls were built, Julie and the kids moved into the yurt and finished putting the roof on while living in it.

"Building the yurt gave a sense of pride to our family," she continues. "It gave me skills and confidence, and I know it helped my children. The two older children did the roof, for example. I kept falling off, and they were simply better at it. My youngest one at three became the supervisor. She would stand there and say, 'Mom says to do this . . .'"

The summer spent building the yurt remains one of their fondest family memories. "You know, we really put our lives back together with that building. It was the most therapeutic process anyone could go through," says Julie." I can't think of a single thing you could do that is better for a child, especially a grieving child, than to build a house together."

PROPORTION AND BEAUTY:
BILL COPERTHWAITE AND DAN NEUMEYER

"There's no particular beauty in a round building—no more than a square building—if the proportions aren't right. The aesthetics and proportion are important factors for me. Some builders can just throw up a round building and be happy with it, but I can't. The proportion has to be just right."

—Bill Coperthwaite

Bill Coperthwaite has had many apprentices over the years. Dan Neumeyer was the youngest of them all. When Dan was ten years old, his father, a Harvard professor, took the family to visit Bill at Dickinson's Reach. An enchanted Dan persuaded his parents to send him back on a bus the following summer to meet Bill at a yurt-building workshop and then spend a couple of months at his homestead. Dan joined Bill at Dickinson's Reach every summer for the next four years to work along side

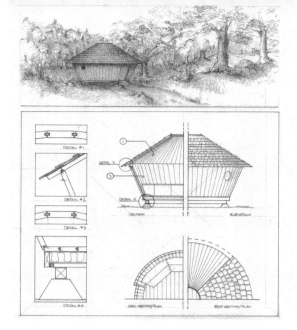

Pictured above are Dan Neumeyer's sketches and design for the Jewel Yurt, which he built at his property on Whidbey Island in Washington State. Dan suggests making lots of sketches as part of any design process, starting with the building and its surroundings before moving on to details.

him. Dan learned skills from canoeing to carving. He also met an extraordinary assortment of people who came for workshops and to visit Bill.

Following high school and during his years as a design student at UC Berkeley, Dan stayed in touch with Bill and, in 1993, accompanied him on a trip to Siberia to collect and learn about native crafts. Today, Dan follows in Bill's footsteps as a designer and builder on Whidbey Island in Washington State. Despite a busy schedule of family and business obligations, Dan visits Dickinson's Reach a couple of times each year to spend time with Bill and remain involved in his life and work.

"A well-proportioned building has a sense of wholeness that we recognize intuitively," Dan says, reflecting Bill's viewpoint. "Indigenous design exhibits this sense of wholeness. Modern design, on the other hand, often misses the intuitive sense of right proportion or right balance."

Some of the reasons for this deficiency in modern design arise from practical considerations. Dan explains: "One of the major challenges in shaping buildings in today's world is the contractual separation between design and construction. There are reasons for preparing a thoroughly defined design before construction begins. This allows a builder to determine just how many board feet a project will require and how many weeks of construction it will take. It allows a buyer to know how much the project will cost."

"What is lost is the opportunity for reflection during the process. The truth is that what is being built has the potential to inform the design as it takes shape. For example, when the walls start to go up, the builder might get a better sense of where the windows ought to go. Once a room is taking shape, one can visualize more clearly how color and detailing will affect the feel."

The ultimate example of proportion lies in nature. The proportion of a leaf to the tree on which it hangs, of the seed to a sunflower, and the lines and proportions of a weeping willow tree–these are things that are only beginning to be grasped in human terms.[*] "There are systems and guidelines from nature like the Golden Mean," says Dan, "and one can start moving toward a balanced proportion by using these guidelines. But ultimately the test is the sense of wholeness and the feeling of balance that proportion gives–which may coincide with somebody's rules, or not. Also, there may not be one particular right proportion but a cluster or set of proportions that feel right. If I'm carving a spoon and you are, they may wind up different but we may each find that field of wholeness."

According to Bill, "Proportion isn't something that can be taught; it may be more of a natural talent or sensibility. The most important thing is to encourage more people to think about good design, good proportion, and beauty. Leaving design to the specialists is like leaving manual skills to the specialists or intellectual pursuits to specialists. It impoverishes us."

"I don't know why I like the proportions I get in yurts," Bill continues, "but a lot of it comes from playing with design. I think this sensibility develops when one spends a lot of time looking at something and saying, 'This line looks better over here than over there.' It eventually becomes intuitive. The only way I know to do it is to work with it, keep playing with it, eventually designing a better yurt, or a better automobile, and moving on to create a better society."

For owner-builders wanting to incorporate proportion into their design process, Dan recommends some basic architectural practices. Using this four-step process can help even novice builders achieve a stronger sense of balance and proportion in their designs.

1. First, try sketching the idea numerous times, each time working to capture the essence.
2. When satisfied with the general sense of wholeness in your sketches, move on to drawing elevations, cross sections, and details. At each level, test for balance, proportion, and wholeness.
3. It's important to visualize the setting. For example, owner-builders might work from photos of the site to sketch it. An understanding of an area and its features can help determine how long and tall a building should be and how much overhang it should have.
4. Finally, creating a three-dimensional model can help owner-builders get a feel for the proportions and balance of their structure. "I often build quick mock-ups," says Dan, "not just to help a client understand what we intend, but also to actually help us in the design process."

Dan points out a couple of factors that contribute to the special qualities of tapered wall yurts. "The aspect of yurt proportion that leads to the 'ahh' factor (what makes people smile as they look at a yurt nestled in a field) is the roof and the way it comes down nearer the ground; it doesn't tower above but is human scale. A nice overhanging eave helps reduce the mass of the building and makes it feel smaller. Inside, the row of windows leads one's eye outward, creating a sense of spaciousness."

Bill has worked for over forty years on yurt design, which has allowed him to fine tune his intuitive understanding of proportion and design. "It's really true that the more of a particular design you do, the more you learn," Bill says. "I learn something new with each yurt I work on. I try to make all of them a little different so that they stay interesting."

"Each time Bill sees a design manifest," adds Dan, "he tries something different, either pushing a dimension more or striving for lines that better capture the sense of wholeness imagined. He has done this so many times that he empirically knows now what angle will feel right from floor to wall, or wall to roof, or how long the eaves want to be."

In Bill Coperthwaite's body of work, the genius of indigenous yurt design, his intimate connection with the natural world, and his finely honed sense of proportion and beauty come together in a unique collection of buildings that exemplify balanced proportion and thoughtful design. Fortunately, apprentices like Dan Neumeyer are walking in Bill's footsteps and continuing the emphasis on proportion, balance, and beauty with their own unique designs.

BILL COPERTHWAITE: A JOURNEY IN DESIGN

Uses for Bill Coperthwaite's yurts have included homes, studios, schools, and retreat and meditation centers. Bill himself has taken the lead in building over three hundred yurts, some of them quite extraordinary designs. These move far beyond the simple versions that an owner-builder might attempt from Bill's plans. Many of them require the mind of a mathematician and each is an expression of the designer's unfolding journey.

Bill's early yurts, as he transitioned away from the portable lattice wall, were strongly experimental. One of the first yurts had parabolic walls and a living roof. "Each board had to be twisted into place," Bill explains. "It was difficult to hold the pieces and control the shape. It was a fun yurt to build, but not easy."

Another early yurt was built at Radcliffe College in Cambridge, Massachusetts, and had a folded plate, or chevron-style, sod roof. In Japan, a workshop group built a seventeen-foot-diameter guesthouse yurt out of tongue-and-groove cedar boards. The tongue-and-groove cedar became standard for many of Bill's yurts that followed. At a church camp in Hunt, Texas, Bill experimented with the "flung" (flying and hung) roof, which requires no tapering of the roof boards.

In the 1970s, *Mother Earth News* magazine owned a large piece of land in Pisgah Forest, North Carolina, where they experimented with research projects in natural building, alternative energy, and gardening. Bill built four yurts at the Mother Earth News property, including the fifty-four-foot-diameter Arabesque Yurt, an experiment using stucco with chopped fiberglass reinforcement for the walls and

A workshop group builds a yurt with parabolic walls, to which they later added a living roof. "It was a fun yurt to build," says Bill, "but not easy."

This early yurt with a folded-plate living roof was built at Radcliffe College in Cambridge, Massachusetts.

The first "flung" (flying and hung) roof, in Hunt, Texas. Note the unusual windows and the rounded door frame.

Inside the first concentric yurt with a folded-plate roof at the University of Massachusetts at Amherst. The bottom part of the inner yurt is visible above the seating area on the right.

Workshop participants build a guesthouse yurt in Japan out of tongue-and-groove cedar boards. This style is typical of a number of yurts that followed.

roof, interspersed with large expanses of glass. "This yurt feels like it's smiling, even dancing," comments Bill.

A number of yurt builders came together to build a yurt for Helen Nearing, widow of Scott Nearing, at the Nearing homestead in Maine. The yurt was built of two-inch tongue-and-groove cedar in a style similar to the Japan yurt but with cupola on top.

Bill continues to explore and integrate different design ideas with each yurt he builds. Recent projects include a bamboo yurt in Arunachal Pradesh, India, built under the auspices of the organization

This concentric yurt built at the Mother Earth News property at Pisgah Forest in North Carolina was featured in articles in the magazine.

One of Bill Coperthwaite's favorite yurts, the fifty-four-foot Arabesque Yurt "feels like it's smiling." The walls and roof are composed of stucco with chopped fiberglass reinforcement, interspersed with large expanses of glass. In the background is another of the four yurts that Bill built at the Mother Earth News property in North Carolina in the 1970s.

This fifty-four-foot-diameter yurt was one of two built by Bill Coperthwaite at the Woodlands Research Institute in South Carolina. It combines an inner raised concentric yurt with an outer "flung"-style roof.

The Dining Yurt at Woodlands Research Institute was Bill Coperthwaite's first thirty-five-foot free-span yurt.

The Nearing Yurt was built by a group of yurt builders at the former Nearing homestead in Maine, now a land trust keeping alive the memory of the life and work of Scott and Helen Nearing. The Nearings were considered by many to be the grandfather and grandmother of the 1960s "back to the land" movement. The yurt is similar to the tongue-and-groove cedar Japan Yurt (see page 55), but with a cupola on top.

The construction of a thirty-five-foot free-span bamboo yurt as a health education center in northeast India. The use of a trellis roof structure dispenses with the need for a central compression ring.

Future Generations for use as a health-education center. With this design, Bill returns to his original yurt modification, the trellis roof, which dispenses with the need for a central ring. And back in California, a newly built whimsical treehouse yurt seems to hang suspended in the forest. Behind each design, from the practical to the fanciful, lies Bill's search for the essence of balance and proportion in design and his quest to unlock and apply "the secrets of the beauty of folk architecture."

The first tapered wall treehouse yurt seems to glow with its own natural light.

THE NANCE FAMILY PROJECT:
A TRI-CENTRIC YURT

"Having a fine house can be a matter of status, of expense and extravagance, or it can mean having the best house for you and your needs, a home that you design and build, a home that is fine because it is simply just right."

—Bill Coperthwaite, *A HANDMADE LIFE*

In the mid-1960s, while living in a "suburban box" in Orange County, California, John Nance began dreaming about building his own house. He imagined a structure that would combine the simplicity of a Japanese teahouse with the roundness of a tipi, geodesic dome, or yurt. "I was convinced that being outside the box would enhance social interactions," says John.

In 1970, the Nance family moved to Polk County, Oregon, in the heart of the fertile Willamette Valley. There they purchased thirteen acres of steeply sloped forest land, miles from the nearest town.

The family's decision to build a yurt rather than a dome was motivated by both site and design considerations. The trees on the land could be made

into a yurt more easily than a dome, and John felt that "the spaces laid out better in the yurt with walls that leaned out, rather than the dome with its inward leaning walls."

John bought sample plans from the Yurt Foundation and traveled around Oregon visiting yurts. The family sketched ideas on paper, evolving a three-story yurt design. Eldest son Jay built a model and the family studied it. John says, "The idea of using poles from the foundation to the upper roof came at that time. We changed our model to integrate and test the new ideas."

"In the design," says John, "I sought to balance centripetal and centrifugal forces by using opposing cones. This allows the weight to be carried along the outer edges, meaning that the interior walls don't have to be load bearing."

Before moving onto the land, the Nances fabricated panels off-site for a twenty-two-foot-diameter straight-walled wooden yurt. They bolted the yurt together on location and used it, along with two travel trailers, as their home during the years it took to build the larger yurt.

To create the superstructure for their tri-centric yurt, the Nances poured a reinforced concrete foundation and embedded railroad rails to anchor two sets of eight leaning poles each, which support the outer edges of the two roofs.

John's greatest building challenge came from an inspector who decided he wanted an engineering study done on the design. John's son Jay finally produced a set of specifications for the yurt years later while getting his degree in engineering.

The Nances selectively harvested trees from their land for the structure. A neighbor with a portable mill turned logs into lumber in exchange for additional logs. "Anything from a two-by-eight up, we milled," says John. "We also rough cut fir boards for siding, which produced a nice exterior."

To create the superstructure, the Nances embedded railroad rails into a reinforced concrete foundation. Eight forty-foot poles were suspended from a central tower and anchored to the railroad rails. These leaning poles supported the outside edge of the top grain bin roof, the center of which rested on the central tower.

The upper roof on this original yurt is a thirty-six-foot-diameter aluminum silo roof. The entry to the left leads from a mudroom into the spacious kitchen and adjoining living room on the main floor.

"The use of opposing cones has allowed for some dramatic interior spaces," observes John Nance. "From the stairwell one can view all three floors and the core of the building's structure. The feeling is like being in a sailing ship complete with masts, beams, and deck."

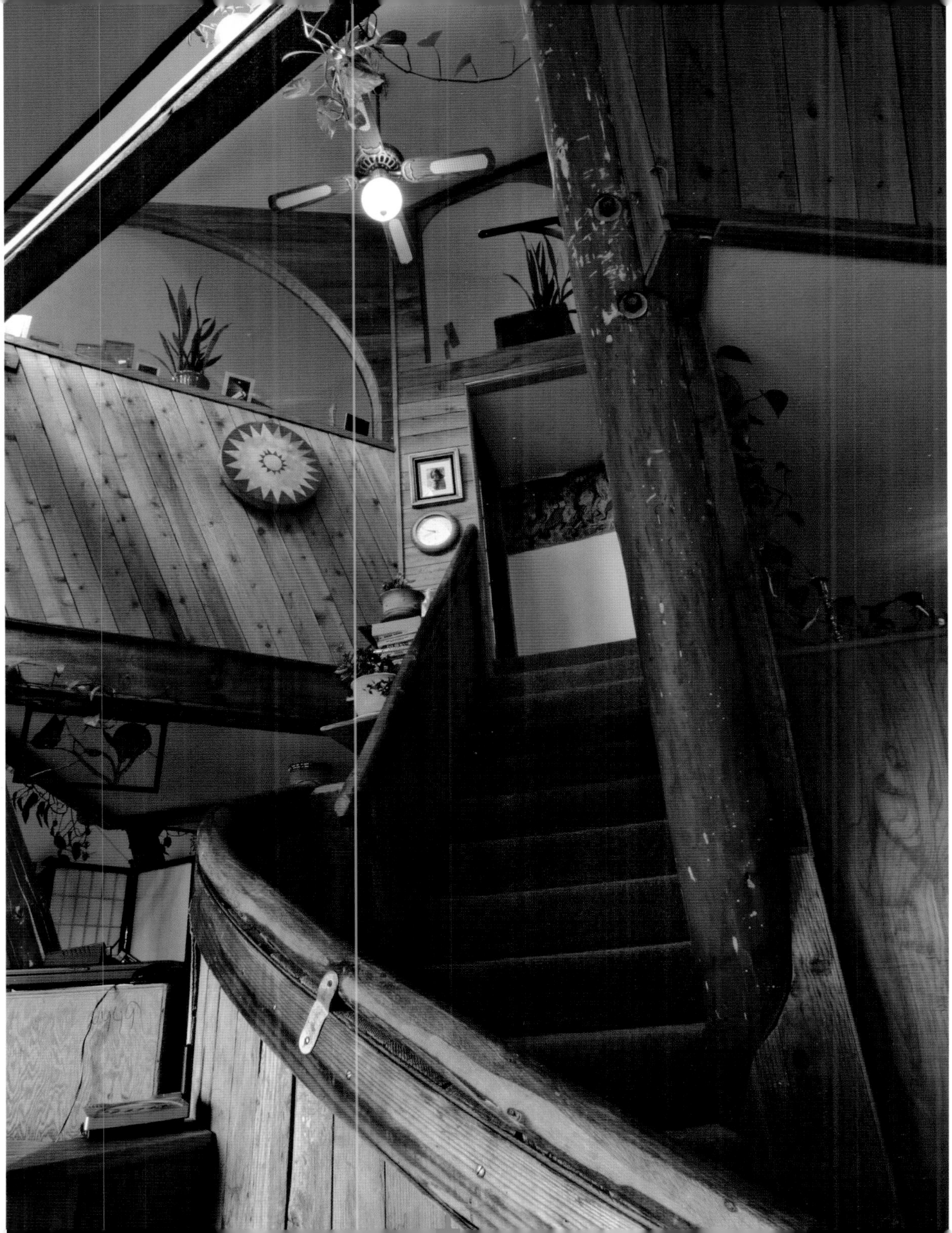

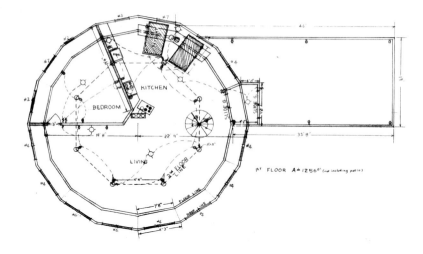

This floor plan of the Nance home shows the mudroom (top right) leading into the expansive kitchen and living areas. It also shows a pie-shaped bedroom located on the level above.

The lower grain bin roof was anchored at its top to the eight forty-foot poles and at its perimeter to an additional set of eight outward-leaning poles. Floor joists on both floors were attached to the central column and the perimeter poles. The middle floor used the angled poles that protrude through it for additional stability.

One advantage of this yurt design was that the building's superstructure came together quickly, enabling the roof to go on early in the process. "Inside work is preferable in our rainy Oregon winters," says John.

"This design for an integrated three-story yurt is unique," John continues. "Many of the ceilings have interesting shapes. The rooms lay out as wedges, with leaning-out exterior walls. We softened the leaning effect by ample use of vertical cabinets against the walls So, despite some initial challenges with furnishings and cabinetry, the end results have been pleasing."

"My work as a psychologist is very stressful," John confides. "Our home is a retreat and a sanctuary. I need separation between my clients and my family, and the yurt provides a radically different environment. My office is a box, which works well for counseling—it is traditional, expected, and safe. At home in the yurt, though, I am outside of the box. The yurt provides me with the sense of separation and change of consciousness that I need."

Like Julie Pratt, John feels that building with family was a positive experience. "There is a feeling of success in having brought the design to fruition. Each member of the family has been affected by the yurt, and being raised in the yurt keeps each member anchored to it. Our children do not want the family's stewardship of the yurt to end with Pat and me. Plans for the next generation's occupancy are in place."

"If you have the opportunity to build your own home, take it," John continues. "If you aren't independently wealthy, the choice is between taking out large loans to have professionals build the house or taking more time and building it yourself as you have the funds. The former approach will get the structure complete while your family is still young; the latter makes it more of a family project."

"In either case, visualize the house as you want it to be. Draw up plans and make layouts. I recommend that you construct a model and work with this to visualize the whole. Try flipping your reference point and working with the spaces contained within the walls, rather than the container. Imagine the pattern of movement through the spaces and the natural flow of energy through the structure."

"I wish we could have finished the project sooner," John muses, "but the building journey itself has been rewarding. It has been a blessing to be able to choose our land, design the structure, and build it our own way."

"The spaces contained by round structures versus boxes create different dynamics. Movement patterns differ. The circle reflects the movement of the moon, planets, the universe, atoms, and the seasons. The circle is a dance, an arc. There are few straight lines in nature, and fewer boxes. Boxes are a contrived form that enhances the industrial style of thinking. They can be aligned and connected, like an organization; the form of the box is very left brain. Circles, on the other hand, are more harmonious with right-brain activity."

–John Nance

"It is enjoyable living in this space," says John Nance. "The rooms lay out pleasantly. The kitchen and living room make good social areas. The bedrooms are quiet and private. From the perspective of feng shui, the chi flows well through the space. The yurt has met our expectations."

THE MODERN FABRIC YURT

"Is it not remarkable that the nomads, while building nonpermanent shelter, have a building tradition that is more durable than ours? The designs of the nomad tents have survived the centuries that have seen great stone monuments turn to dust. If these tents have sheltered a portion of mankind so well in the past, might they not be useful in the future?"

—Torvald Faegre, *Tents: Architecture of the Nomads*

The modern fabric yurt retains the nomadic character of the Mongolian ger but steps into the clothing of the twenty-first century. The trellis wall still holds everything up, and the roof struts still rise to a wooden center ring. But now, instead of a horsehair rope circling the trellis wall, a steel-cable tension band rests on the crosses (or heads) at the top of the trellis. The roof struts are no longer lashed to the trellis wall but are notched and rest on the aircraft cable.

The smoke hole, with its felted cover, has metamorphosed into an acrylic skylight bubble, which can be raised to increase airflow or lowered to keep in heat. Instead of an open fire in the middle, a woodstove or propane heater now warms the yurt.

The felted wool outer covering, unsuitable for moist climates, has been replaced by architectural fabric, chosen from a multitude of fireproof, waterproof, and mildew-resistant material and coating options. Instead of "white ger" and "black ger," yurts now come in beige, forest green, terra-cotta red, and even indigo blue.

The insulating properties of felted wool have been replaced by NASA-developed space insulation, a sandwich of plastic bubble wrap

TOP: This colorful woodland yurt has French doors and lots of picture windows.

BOTTOM: The fabric yurt, an updated version of the Mongolian ger, uses modern materials and a stream-lined design. It remains relatively portable and can be erected or dismantled in a day.

between two layers of reflective aluminum coating. Modern yurt dwellers still add their own rugs and quilted wall hangings, paralleling the carpets and fine wall pieces used by the nomads for both decoration and insulation.

The Central Asian yurt is dark and womblike. In contrast, the modern fabric yurt with its multiple windows and skylight bubble feels airy and full of light. Windows can be screened for ventilation or have outside flaps that convert to awnings, or they can be picture-window size. Doors come in all shapes and sizes: glass panels, screened curtains, and double French doors are available.

The fabric yurt isn't as mobile as its Mongol ancestor. Instead of thirty to sixty minutes, putting up a modern fabric yurt takes a full day. The outer covering attaches to a permanent wooden platform; the yurt no longer rests on the ground. But compared to the time and energy that goes into a site-built house with a thirty-year mortgage, the modern fabric yurt is still a relatively portable, accessible, and affordable solution for the modern family.

A mélange of brightly colored yurts dot the landscape at this girl scout camp in Tulsa, Oklahoma.

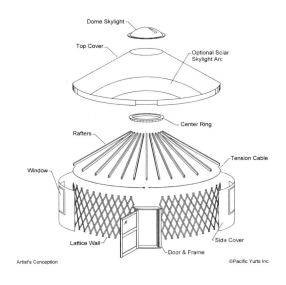

Dome Skylight
Top Cover
Optional Solar Skylight Arc
Center Ring
Rafters
Tension Cable
Window
Lattice Wall
Side Cover
Door & Frame
Artist's Conception
©Pacific Yurts Inc.

This diagram shows all the parts that come with a basic fabric yurt package and how they fit together. Insulation is added between the structural components (trellis wall and rafters) and the fabric covering.

THE YURT STORY: ORIGINS OF THE FABRIC YURT

Chuck Cox was a student in Bill Coperthwaite's high school math class in 1962 when Bill got interested in the Mongolian ger and had the class build the first experimental yurt roof. Chuck went on to study at Cornell University and, for his senior project, built a portable trellis-walled yurt with bentwood (Turkic-style) roof struts and a canvas cover.

After Chuck married, he and his wife, Laurel (also a student of Bill Coperthwaite's), lived in Chuck's portable yurt in Alaska, New York, and then at a Quaker boarding school in Rindge, New Hampshire. There they built four more fabric yurts for use as student housing and produced a set of plans called *The Portable Yurt*.

The plans used Mongolian-style straight roof rafters since they were simpler to make than bentwood struts. The rafters were notched and sat on a tension ring of steel aircraft cable. Chuck's center ring was a layered, offset octagonal design (made of two-by-fours or two-by-sixes), a design still used by yurt companies today. It was topped with an eight-sided Plexiglas skylight, used in all the early fabric yurts and still used for some back-country applications.

When *The Portable Yurt* came out in the late 1960s, the "back to the land" movement was in full swing and people were looking for ways to create their own shelters. Chuck and Laurel's plans became part of the movement. Among the early yurt pioneers was a Wyoming couple who used the plans to build yurts and start a yurt community near Jackson Hole, Wyoming. In Oregon, a hippie tree-planting cooperative called the Hoedads modified the plans for forest use, and the yurt became a symbol of their movement.[1]

backcountry yurts

College student Kirk Bachman used the Coxes' plans to build a portable yurt as a senior project. After graduation, he took the yurt with him to work as a backcountry guide in the mountains of Idaho. Kirk's employer was a pioneer in backcountry hut-to-hut ski systems. When he asked Kirk to build some yurts as hut replacements, the backcountry yurt movement was born.

After some of his original yurts caved in under snow, Kirk modified the Coxes' plans to meet the intense snow-load requirements of the area. Kirk used hand-peeled lodgepole pine to make stronger rafters and removed the rafter pin from the design, inserting the rafter itself into the center ring as the Mongolians do. He also alternated the grain on the offset octagonal rings that make up the center ring and fiberglassed the entire ring to add strength. Kirk's yurt company, Outback Yurts, has continued making backcountry-style yurts on a limited basis. Each yurt is a custom creation, sometimes including window frames with thermal-pane glass windows.[2]

Brothers Jeff and Bo Norris saw an article about Kirk's yurts and started their own East Coast hut-to-hut yurt business that produced many Nordic yurts and yurt homes before going out of business in 2000.

evolution of the fabric yurt

Alan Bair first lived in a yurt as a Hoedad tree planter. He loved the design and caught a vision for producing affordable, sustainable shelter to meet a broad range of needs. With some friends, he started Centering Shelterworks in a barn in the Oregon countryside, later buying out his friends and continuing as Pacific Yurts. Alan developed the yurt from the Coxes' simple, rustic, canvas-covered structure into the finished-looking manufactured product that Pacific Yurts produces today, with NASA insulation, architectural fabrics, a skylight bubble, and a streamlined, contemporary aesthetic style.

Custom-built Outback Yurts use hand-peeled lodgepole pine logs for rafters and keep the rustic feel of the early fabric yurt designs.

One of Jerry Gray's early solar yurt designs, this Colorado ski-hut yurt uses clear plastic on its south-facing side to increase solar gain during the day. Clip-in thermal insulation helps contain heat during the night. The solar roof pictured here has not been utilized in later designs.

Other yurt makers and designers have added their unique touches. Yacht-builder Will Hayes created a unique center ring when he and Jenny Pell started Nesting Bird Yurts in 1994. Current owner Scott Campbell (who renamed the company Rainier Yurts) brings the expertise of parent company Rainier Industries, which started making wall tents in 1896 for Alaska miners and today manufactures fabric products for corporate clients.

Another early designer was Arizona tipi-maker Blue Evening Star, who combined tipi and yurt design into a unique Southwest-style yurt. She also wrote the first book on fabric yurts, *Building Tipis and Yurts*, and held workshops that taught people to make their own yurts.

Dan and Emma Kiger also started as tipi makers (see their story on page 98). They pursued modern yurt design for mountain dwellers with their Colorado Yurt Company, later growing to serve a worldwide clientele and adding some unique options.

Another tipi maker turned yurt designer is Jerry Gray, whose yurts have been popping up in the Colorado hut system since 1991. The mission of Jerry's company, Red Mountain Lodge Works, is "to adapt solar design and modern materials to ancient dwellings." Jerry's yurts have an unusual south-facing open front covered in clear heavy-duty plastic that brings in the sun's warmth during the day. Clip-in window insulation keeps the warmth

Owner-builders Dan Beck and Kris Ernst lived in this yurt with their two children while building their house. Now that they live in their house, they miss the yurt. "Living in a yurt," says Dan, "brings you back to what it feels to be human and connected to your family and to your world."

contained once the sun goes down. The yurts are designed to be transported on cross-country skis and set up after the first snow.

Canadian company Yurtco has followed Kirk Bachman's lead in using lodgepole pine rafters for added roof strength, but at commercial production levels. A major focus for Yurtco has been the park system and camping businesses, for which their sister company, Canadian Yurts, offers long-term yurt rentals.

One final design innovation is a true camping yurt, designed by Howie Oaks of GoYurt Shelters. Using ultra-lightweight materials and some unique design innovations, the thirteen- and sixteen-foot GoYurts are as portable as most tents and can be set up by two people in thirty minutes.

YURT USES

The possible uses for these fabric shelters are almost endless. Owner-builders can live on-site in their yurt, in comfort, while they build a dream house at their own speed. This provides the opportunity to get to know the site–where the wind blows and the water flows, how the sun affects the site as it moves through the seasons, where the cold spots are, and where the best garden and orchard sites might be–all before starting to build.

When the house is finished, the yurt can become a guest room, office, studio, or meditation space. It can also be sold and shipped to a new owner. Sometimes, though, the original yurt turns out to be so comfortable that the site-built house never gets built.

Biology professors Dan Beck and Kris Ernest lived in a yurt for four years while building their house near Ellensburg, Washington. "Our son was just born and our daughter was three when we moved into the yurt," reminisces Dan. "We all slept in a loft together on two futons. We loved living in the yurt."

"Our extra stuff went into storage and it felt like we had everything we needed in that one large space," Dan continues. "Now that our house is built, we've sold the yurt to a family in Indiana, but I have to admit that we miss it. Living in a yurt brought us back to what it feels like to be human and connected–to our family and to our world. In a yurt, you can *feel* what's going on in the world outside. You also become aware, when you're bringing in wood for a fire, of how much of the world's resources you're using; you become more mindful. For us, the combination of the yurt, our kids, and building a house brought a strong sense of connections."

Homeowners may choose to use a yurt instead of building an addition or an outbuilding. Sometimes this is a matter of economy or a way to deal with building code limitations; sometimes it's simply because they prefer the feel of the yurt.

Los Angeles home-designer Jeff Suhy put a yurt in his backyard when his wife was expecting their first child. "After we put the yurt up, my mother came to visit for a few months to help with the baby," Jeff explains, "so we put her in the yurt. Three years later she was still in the yurt and didn't want to leave. She said it was the nicest space she had ever lived in."

The modern fabric yurt also makes a perfect vacation home, requiring minimal input for maximum "back to nature" enjoyment. Instead of investing years into financing and building a perfect getaway cabin, a family can build a deck and put up a yurt in the first weeks of the summer and then spend the rest of their time vacationing and enjoying their land.

For businesses, the modern fabric yurt can provide an affordable office, selling space, or artist's studio that is easily set up. Often used as a starter space, the yurt sometimes proves so workable that it is adopted as a permanent solution.

This thirty-foot yurt in the Utah mountains makes a wonderful getaway from the hustle and bustle of the city. "Being in a yurt feels like you're outdoors without being outdoors," says yurt designer Will Hayes. "You have the comfort and security of shelter without losing intimacy with the natural environment."

Bay Area mosaic artist Debra Amerson crafted this mosaic backing for the woodstove in her Myurt office and artist's studio. Note the use of a screen on the right to provide privacy.

When Gabrielle Tiradani moved to the Ocean Song community in Occidental, California, this handmade yurt became her instant artist's studio.

Sacred Groves eco-retreat center on Bainbridge Island near Seattle uses this yurt as a Moonlodge (a retreat space for women on their moon time) and a space for women's gatherings.

Artist Debra Amerson first encountered yurts at a weeklong artist's workshop on the California coast. When she and her partner bought a house in West Marin County, California, Debra realized she wanted her own studio and found herself repeatedly saying to her friends, "When I get 'My Yurt' . . . " She hired some locals who had experience with yurts and together they built a deck on top of eight-foot concrete-filled Sonotube columns with a stone retaining wall. In front of the yurt, they built a raised garden bed for bamboo.

When Debra got her yurt, she named her design business Myurt in its honor. A Chilean shaman visited to bless the yurt, and twenty-two friends gathered in a circle under the skylight to offer prayers for the space. Debra uses the yurt as her office and creative art space, but the yurt also has hosted mid-winter yoga classes, business groups, trainings, and meetings of the West Marin Women's Brain Exchange. "People love coming here for business meetings," says Debra. "I love my yurt, and I love sharing it with people."

The framework of the yurt is incredibly strong. There is an old story about Kazakh hunters who would crawl inside a yurt frame, lift it up on stakes, and carry it with them to track tigers. When they got within gunshot range of a tiger, they would lower the frame and wait for the tiger to attack the yurt, at which point the tiger would be met with blows of lances and sabers and pointblank gunshots. Even if the tiger leaped onto the dome of the yurt, the dome rods would bear the tiger's weight and keep the hunters safe.

Lee Tenhof of Nomad Shelter in Alaska tells stories of Alaskan bears trying to break into yurts without success. But yurt-builder and backcountry-guide Kirk Bachman has a yurt in the high country of central Idaho that attracts a passing bear every spring. The bear has damaged the yurt in the past but, since the yurt is unoccupied when the bear comes through, Kirk leaves the door open every spring and then cleans up after the bear (rather than risk more damage to the yurt).

If you live in bear country, you might want to build your deck up high. A mountain couple I know used this tactic. They felt it helped them avoid problems with the numerous bears on their property. However, Karie Knoke (see the first chapter) had a bear climb up onto her eight-foot-high deck and take numerous swipes at the side of her yurt. The bear didn't break through the trellis wall, but Karie did have to replace torn fabric (see photo below).

Yurt companies have various solutions they recommend to customers. Canada's Yurtco suggests using bear boards, "an example of northern ingenuity." Bear boards are pieces of plywood with nails or wood screws poking through that are placed at potential access points with the nails facing out (or up, as the case may be). They have to be large enough so that the bear can only get access to the yurt by stepping on the boards. Colorado Yurt Company customers have used electric fences, finding them effective at deterring bears without harming the bears.[3]

So, in bear country, consider a high deck and use bear boards at access points. If the problem persists, try an electric bear fence. Store food properly and keep your yurt clean to avoid attracting bears. The trellis wall of the yurt will keep you protected, but if bears do rip through the fabric, the component construction of a yurt makes repairs quick and cost effective.

The damage was caused by a bear trying to break into Karie Knoke's yurt in north Idaho (see the first chapter). The bear tore the fabric in a number of places but wasn't able to break through the lattice wall. Karie repaired the damaged sections with fabric supplied by her yurt company.

sandpoint waldorf school in north idaho

Smiling children carry musical instruments, artwork, and novellas of their own making through the halls of the Waldorf school in Sandpoint, Idaho. Today the school is housed in a handsome two-story building with plenty of room for over one hundred students enrolled in preschool through eighth grade. But it wasn't always that way. It started, like many Waldorf schools, with a small group of parents who wanted an alternative learning experience for their children.

"We chose fabric yurts as our first classrooms for aesthetic, health, and financial reasons," says Susan Prez, one of the founders. "Our other option was modular classrooms. We didn't like the feel of the modular units and realized the materials used to make them were pretty toxic. We didn't want our children in that environment. The yurts were also reasonably priced."

The parents worked to get building code approval for the yurts; they involved the whole community in the project and overcame numerous hurdles. "We had to have good insulation and good furnaces," says Susan. "We used two propane heaters on opposite sides of the room, and a fan to circulate the air."

"The yurts made great classrooms," Susan continues. "I remember that the rain was loud on the roofs, and could be distracting, but it doesn't rain that much here. After six years we had outgrown the yurts and built ourselves a new building, so we sold the yurts and sent them off to another organization."

Yurts have also been used as facilities for outdoor education programs. At the Canyonlands Field Institute campus near Moab, Utah, campers stay in tipis, listen to lectures in a classroom yurt, and get their meals in a kitchen yurt. The camp is located on leased land, and the yurts have allowed the camp to meet their lease requirement of temporary structures.

Canyonlands Field Institute near Moab, Utah, helps people experience nature through hiking, camping, and river running. Campers stay in tipis. Cooking and classes take place in these two yurts.

The kitchen yurt is one of two Canyonlands Field Institute yurts originally purchased in 1988. The fabric for both yurts was replaced in 1999, which allowed for upgrading and custom modifications.

cedar House Inn and Yurts in the Georgia Woods
Fred and Mary Beth Tanner renovated a local landmark in Dahlonega, Georgia, to create the Cedar House Inn and Yurts bed and breakfast. Wanting to provide more than just the inn, they researched eco-friendly structures and found yurts. Yurts offered a number of advantages for the Tanners. The yurt's classification as a "temporary structure" resolved potential code issues on their three acres. Yurts were also affordable and easy to erect.

In 2002, the Tanners purchased two yurts and furnished them with queen-sized beds, mini fridges, coffee makers, and electric heaters. They equipped each yurt with a composting toilet and built a small bathhouse with sinks and showers within walking distance from both yurts. Yurt guests are invited to the inn dining room each morning for steaming coffee and a full country breakfast.

"The yurts have been a great success for us," says Fred Tanner. "They paid for themselves in just two years. If we had it to do over again, we probably wouldn't even renovate the rooms in the house; we'd just go with the yurts. We've noticed, though, that people who don't know yurts sometimes are hesitant to stay in them. They stay in our inn rooms and then take a look at the yurts while they're here. They usually decide to stay in the yurts for their next visit."

The Tanners have found that their yurts often remain occupied during slow times when their competitors' cabins are empty. "I'm surprised that more people aren't doing what we're doing," says Fred. "The yurts are an easy entry into the business, and they're not that hard to set up. And the yurts are unique, which is probably why they're always full, even during cold weather."

Yurts like this one at Falling Waters Resort (see page 76) are growing in popularity at resorts, retreat centers, and bed and breakfasts.

Guests at Cedar House Inn and Yurts are welcomed into yurts furnished with queen-sized beds, coffee makers, and mini fridges. Breakfast is served each morning at the inn.

Like the Tanners, Falling Waters Resort loves their yurts. Parent company Whitewater Ltd. Rafting is a family business leading whitewater rafting tours on South Carolina's Chattooga River (setting for the movie *Deliverance*). After successfully renting out cabins at their rafting headquarters, the company decided to branch out. In 1998, they opened Falling Waters Resort on twenty-two wooded acres in North Carolina's Smoky Mountains. They started with four eighteen-foot-diameter yurts, each furnished with beds for four and equipped with a small refrigerator, coffee maker, and private deck. The next year the resort added four more yurts and a group lodge for church groups and family reunions.

"We went with the yurts because they were different," says Carolyn Allison, marketing liaison. "This area is saturated with cabins, from the high-end designer types to cabins that are quite rustic. The yurts stand out because they are unique. They also fill the need for a place between cabins and camping. In a yurt, you can hear the waterfall and the crickets chirping at nightfall without having to sleep on the hard ground or wake up in three inches of water when it rains. We call it 'the experience of camping with the comforts of home.' It's especially good for families or couples where one member is squeamish about camping and the other loves it; this way they can 'camp' and still be comfortable."

Shared guest facilities for the yurts include a bathhouse with private bathrooms, a hot tub, barbeque areas with picnic tables, and a covered picnic pavilion for groups. Most guests cook on barbeques or bring their own camping stoves. If they don't want to cook, there are restaurants nearby.

"We don't keep an innkeeper on-site, and we don't do breakfasts," Carolyn explains. "We have a facilities manager who checks in every day. We put keys out for guests and leave an emergency number where they can call. Most of our guests really appreciate the privacy but some city types are nervous with no 'host' there. This is a camping experience, and it doesn't work for everyone.

"Sixty or seventy percent of the guests come for the rafting. But others come with an armful of books and a bottle or two of wine," says Carolyn. "They're just here to relax. Many of them come back every year and ask for the same yurt. Our group lodge is a sparser dorm-style situation, but it works well with the yurts because groups can rent the lodge and then overflow into the yurts."

The yurts at Falling Waters Resort in North Carolina's Smoky Mountains provide a good middle ground between comfort and camping. Another advantage is that the yurts are easier to put up than stick-built cabins. "Because they're on a deck and not a foundation," says marketing manager Carolyn, "we had a lot of flexibility in working them into the natural landscape, and we didn't have to take out trees."

Twinkling lights greet visitors alighting from a sleigh to feast at the Viking Yurt Restaurant, high on a ski mountain in Park City, Utah.

The atmosphere inside the restaurant is festive, with candles and live piano music accompanying the multicourse gourmet dinner.

THE VIKING YURT RESTAURANT IN PARK CITY, UTAH
In the winter of 1998, Joy and Geir Vik opened the Viking Yurt, a one-of-a-kind restaurant experience in the ski town of Park City, Utah. The yurt restaurant seats thirty-two guests per evening and reservations must be made in advance. Guests meet at an appointed time and travel together, belted in and wrapped in cozy blankets, up one thousand feet in a sleigh pulled by a snow cat. Disembarking from the sleigh at eight thousand feet, guests are greeted by twinkling lights and strains of live piano music wafting from the snow-covered Viking Yurt (so named for the hot, spiced Norwegian glogg and the traditional Norwegian decor that await inside).

A crackling fire in the woodstove warms the thirty-foot yurt as guests mingle and sip glogg around a baby grand piano. The acclaimed house chef works over a propane-fired stove putting the finishing touches on the first course of a gourmet dinner that has arrived at the yurt via snowmobile from the lodge below. Locals take their seats with tourists from around the world. After finishing their five-course meal and enjoying friendly banter and live

music, guests climb back into the sleigh and cuddle in with their blankets for the ride down the hill.

The Viking Yurt has been such a success that in 2003 the Viks added a second smaller yurt, which seats ten to twelve and is ideal for private parties. The sixteen-foot-diameter Yonder Yurt is warmed with a propane heater and serves the same menu but fewer courses than the Viking Yurt, making it a more appropriate venue for children.

The Viks have been delighted with their yurts, their guests are ecstatic about the food, and the media love writing about this unique dining and travel experience.

PRACTICAL CONSIDERATIONS

The modern fabric yurt is an affordable, moveable, flexible, accessible shelter that is easy to erect and has a multitude of uses. It is also, however, an unusual structure, more refined and stable than a wall tent, yet still not the conventional stick-frame, log, or stone house that we may have grown up with. The prospect of living or running a business in one of these "tents" naturally brings up lots of questions.

This section covers some of the most commonly asked questions about living in yurts. The yurt companies' customer-service departments can also answer questions and give more detailed advice about their specific type of yurt.

under the yurt: foundations to flooring

The steppes of Central Asia are very dry, and the nomads set their yurts up directly on the grassy plain. In other parts of the world, if the climate is dry enough, a yurt can also be set up directly on the ground.

A yurt community in Kelly, Wyoming, lived without platforms under their yurts for over twenty years. Here's what they did to make it work: [1] They drove pegs into the ground around the perimeter of the yurt, spaced a distance of four or five trellis "feet" (or bottom crisscrosses) apart. Using rope, the yurt cover was secured to the pegs. (This also helped tighten up the wall fabric and make the yurt less drafty.) [2] They then dug a

This sunny Baja yurt sits on a typical short platform. The deck hangs out over a slope and provides a shaded outdoor room. Even with a platform as short as this one, screened windows can be hard to reach to open for ventilation.

drainage trench around the perimeter of the yurt and filled it with rocks or gravel. [3] The interior yurt floor was dug down six inches, covered with plastic sheeting, and filled in with sawdust or sand. Rugs were placed over the soft sawdust or sand floor. [4] Some villagers built an elevated platform over part of the floor, on which they placed their beds or a seating area. This provided a warmer elevated space in the winter as well as extra storage under the platform.

The most common foundation for yurts is some form of deck or platform. The circular platform should be built the same diameter as the yurt so that the bottom of the yurt covering can be attached to the deck just below floor level. This provides added stability for the whole yurt and creates a strong weather seal.

Most yurt companies include designs for a platform in their set-up instructions; some companies have plans available online. In Appendix 2, you'll find a sample plan for a yurt platform and a sample materials list, but be sure to work with what your yurt company sends and build to the exact measurements they give for your size of yurt. Otherwise the yurt won't be as tight and weatherproof as it is designed to be.[4]

Yurt platforms are usually built at least eighteen to twenty-four inches above the ground to provide a crawl space for installing plumbing and wiring and for use as storage. Some people elevate their yurt platforms a full story—or build on a hillside—to provide additional storage space or an extra room below. With a taller platform, the heat source (propane heater, woodstove, or boiler) may be kept in a room below, leaving more open floor space in the yurt above.

However, by building a higher platform, you may lose access to screened windows, which open from the outside of the yurt. To reach the windows, you will need a walkway or deck around the yurt or a window flap system that can be operated from ground level.[5] Make sure to resolve this problem before you build. A number of yurt owners have built tall or hillside platforms and then not had access to their screened windows for ventilation.

I would discourage building a tall platform unless there is a clear advantage to doing so or you're building a deck around the yurt platform before the yurt goes up, from which there will be easy access to the windows, walls, and roof. Having the platform up high without an accompanying deck makes erecting the yurt (and simple maintenance chores) much more complex because everything has to be accomplished on tall ladders, often on uneven ground.

You might consider building your platform with structural insulated panels (SIPs). These panels have a core of rigid foam insulation in the middle and sheets of oriented strand board (OSB) or plywood laminated to either side of the insulation. The SIPs can be cut to size for your platform by either the manufacturer or your yurt company. SIPs are more expensive than buying plywood and insulation separately, but they insulate well and can simplify the building process.[6]

When adding decking around a yurt, it is important to leave enough space around the circular platform to attach the yurt cover to the platform below floor level. There are two ways to do this: [1] you can build your outer deck at least five inches lower than the yurt platform, or [2] if building the deck and platform on the same level, you can leave enough separation between the yurt platform and outer decking to easily attach the cover.[7] If you are planning to connect your yurt with an existing building, allow at least twelve inches between your deck and the existing building. A covered walkway can be added between the two after the yurt is put up.

Wood platforms aren't the only option for yurt foundations. My favorite yurt had a cob floor with hot springs water piped through it. (Cob is an adobe-like mixture made from clay, sand, and straw.) The floor had a natural, earthy feel and the radiant heat kept the yurt warm and cozy through long, cold winters.

Various materials are available for flooring. Most people use either plywood or tongue-and-groove wood flooring. Both can be attractive with a clear finish. Use screws instead of nails if you think you might move the platform at a future date, and don't forget to place the insulation in the platform before the flooring goes on, unless you have a crawl space and can easily access the underside of the platform after the yurt is installed. A floating laminate floor is also worth considering; it is easy to install and can be moved with the yurt.

In my current yurt, we painted a plywood floor using a "sponging" technique to apply layers of different colors, ending with a clear acrylic finish. The floor looks like linoleum instead of plywood, and the variety of colors adds a sense of depth to the room.

YURTS AND CLIMATE

Probably the most common questions about yurts have to do with hot and cold climates. How do you heat a yurt? Can you insulate a yurt? How do you keep it cool?

siting

The place to start, as you would with any shelter, is siting. Good siting will help with a multitude of climate issues. For example, you can use deciduous trees to keep your yurt cool in the summer without blocking the sun in the winter. If there aren't trees where you place your yurt, consider planting some. You may be there longer than you expect. Trees are also useful in providing a windbreak.

In a desert climate, you may not have access to trees but you will have sunshine through the winter. It's amazing what a difference it makes to orient windows or a glazed door to catch the morning sun and warm up your yurt at the beginning of the day. South-facing windows will bring in the sun's heat in the winter, and tile or adobe floors can store some of that heat and release warmth in the evening. (Be sure to place awnings over those windows for the summer, though.)[8]

staying warm: Heating options

Most conventional heating options will work in a yurt. Even forced-air or central heating can be used, for example, by installing ductwork under the floor of the yurt.

Keep in mind that the tendency with a conical roof is for heat to travel along the roofline to the skylight bubble and then out unless you insulate the skylight, lower the ceiling, or create a way to send heat across the room and back down from the bubble.

WOODSTOVES

Perhaps the best heater for yurts is the wood or pellet stove. Wood creates a dry heat, making a yurt feel warm and cozy in cold, wet climates. Woodstoves aren't permitted in many communities because of air-pollution issues, but, where they are permitted, consider purchasing a newer model. New stoves are highly efficient and re-burn their toxic gasses, producing minimal emissions. Besides providing good heat and being a renewable resource, in many areas wood is the most readily available and economical fuel source.

A common mistake people make is to install a woodstove that is too large for the yurt (being round, yurts are very heat efficient). If the stove is too large for the space, you'll end up closing down the air intake to burn the wood more slowly, which produces a smoky fire, more pollutants, and creosote that will coat your stovepipe and make your stove much less efficient.[9]

In extremely cold climates, the stove is sometimes placed in the middle of the yurt to provide an even heat throughout. This is what the Mongolians have done for millennia and it has been recommended by cold-climate yurt companies. In a bitterly cold climate, this option is worth considering. Alaska's Nomad Shelter sells yurts with an optional skylight designed for this purpose. However, most yurt dwellers prefer to vent their stoves out the side and leave the center floor space open.

Kirk Bachman, backcountry guide and owner of Outback Yurts, has this to say about woodstove placement: "I prefer to locate the stove next to the door for two reasons: [1] Woodstoves operate via drafting air, which means air drafts towards the stove. If the stove is near the door, the drafty feeling is minimized. [2] When the stove is near the door, packing wood into the yurt is more convenient and less messy, especially when you are tracking in snow on your boots."

Fans are highly recommended for circulating heat around a yurt. There are two ways fans can be used: a fan can be placed above or behind the stove and oriented to send heat across the room or a ceiling fan can recirculate the heat that rises to the top, sending it back down and around the room.

Propane and natural gas heaters are used in many yurts, both in cities and in remote locations without access to a good wood supply. Propane heaters are great for schools and kids' camps where safety is an issue; they also work well for dance and yoga studios where the heat source needs to be back against the wall.[10]

One advantage of propane over wood heat is that the thermostat keeps the temperature constant. Even when you are away from your yurt, your pipes won't freeze and the snow will stay melted off your roof. If you live in a cold climate and have to be gone a lot, you might consider using both wood and propane (with the stove and heater on opposite sides of the yurt) to take advantage of the benefits of each. Like woodstoves, propane heaters require a fan to help circulate the heat.

As a primary heat source only *vented* propane heaters should be used and they should be installed by a professional. Unvented heaters (space heaters) should only be used for short periods of time as a secondary heat source (for example, to counteract a morning chill). The by-products of propane combustion are water vapor and carbon monoxide, making unvented heaters inappropriate for use as a primary heat source because of the resulting dampness in the yurt and the danger of carbon monoxide poisoning.

If you're using an unvented propane heater, for

Like much of the yurt movement, using yurts in parks was the idea of a single visionary. Former Oregon Parks and Recreation marketing manager Craig Tutor was looking for a way to make the parks more broadly accessible. Single parents, after working all week and caring for kids, he realized, were too exhausted to pack everything into the car, drive somewhere, and set up a tent. Craig saw a yurt at the Oregon Country Fair and thought, "Why not give it a try?"

Craig went to Alan Bair of Pacific Yurts in Cottage Grove, Oregon, who worked with him to get state approval for yurts as recreational structures.

The first yurts went up at Cape Lookout in 1991 and were an immediate success. As with any new venture, there were, of course, some initial problems to be solved. The early yurts were prone to mold and mildew on the rainy Oregon coast, but Pacific Yurts helped the parks change over to covers with greater mold and mildew resistance.

Oregon Parks started with sixteen-foot yurts in their campgrounds across the state and now offer twenty-four-foot deluxe yurts as well. The deluxe yurts, pictured above left at Umpaqua Campground, have a kitchenette, microwave, TV/VCR combo, and walls that enclose a bathroom and shower. The interior of the deluxe yurt is shown above right and the floor plan is shown below right.

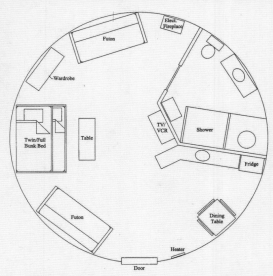

These two yurts were installed in 1995 at Florissant Fossil Beds National Monument in Colorado and have served many functions since. Until 2000, they served as a visitor center and protection for the fossils (top right). From 2000 to 2003, they became classrooms, a storage facility for paleontology items, and a place for showing films to guests. In 2006, they were reinstalled with new custom doors and fabric exteriors for use as classrooms and public gathering spaces. "They're a great space for teaching and workshops," says the director, "because the yurt naturally brings everyone together in a circle."

One side benefit that Oregon Parks discovered was that, by making a few adjustments, yurts could be made wheelchair accessible, thereby opening up camping possibilities to a whole new population. The yurts in Oregon Parks now number over two hundred, and many of them are booked nine months in advance for peak season use. The campgrounds with yurts get more use in the cold off-season months as well.

The parks now offer both the standard sixteen-foot-diameter rustic yurts and twenty-four-foot-diameter deluxe yurts. The deluxe yurts have internal walls that enclose a bathroom and shower, and they also boast a kitchenette, microwave, and a TV/VCR combo. Campers can cook on a big grill outside.

Jean Thompson, manager of public services for Oregon Parks and Recreation, says that they could double the number of yurts and still be just as full. Oregon Parks is not alone in its success with yurts, which have become a national phenomenon in the camping industry as the number of parks and resorts experimenting with yurts across North America continues to grow.

Jean suggests that other camping organizations learn from Oregon Parks' experience. For anyone considering using yurts in a camping rental situation, it's important to know ahead of time that yurts require relatively high maintenance for a campground setting. This is because:

o— they are always in use, seven days a week
o— there's not much turnaround time between occupants
o— yurts require more cleaning than a traditional campsite or RV hookup
o— although people usually follow the rules, they don't always honor cooking, smoking, and dog restrictions

While yurts as a concept should work just about anywhere, Jean suggests doing some information gathering before beginning. For example, park managers can ask people who use their sites what they would like to see, and an organization might poll potential customers who don't currently camp but would camp if they could stay in a yurt."

Oregon Parks has also found it helpful to place log books in the yurts, where people can write about their stay and give feedback. For example, Oregon Parks is reconsidering their "no dogs" rule after receiving feedback from guests who want to bring their dogs. There are also simple helpful things (like installing hooks for coats and towels) that can be overlooked but may be suggested in the log books.

This Colorado Yurt Company yurt seems at home in its park surroundings. Note the thermal-pane glass windows.

any reason, it's a good idea to purchase a carbon monoxide monitor from your local hardware store.

How do propane and wood heat compare? Paul and Criss Fosselman recently switched from propane to wood heat in their thirty-foot yurt in north Idaho. "With propane," says Paul, "it seemed a challenge to keep ourselves warm. We were constantly adding extra insulation, for example, to try to make it work. Our costs were pretty high, too—around a $1,000 to $1,200 per winter. It's a big space to heat. With wood the costs are negligible, since we get the wood off our land. There have been other benefits—getting to know the land better, becoming more self-sufficient, learning to work with wood—and we're much warmer. We were in shorts and T-shirts during a cold spell last winter. Because the wood heat is constant, it seems that everything naturally stays warmer. The propane got to a certain temperature and shut off, creating a constant cycle of burn and cool, burn and cool."

Debra Amerson, the artist whose yurt studio is located in the Bay Area (see page 72), feels differently about the woodstove in her yurt. "The romance of building a fire ended about two months into my time in the yurt," she says. "Woodstoves are messy. We've got a propane stove in the house and I like using it. If I had it to do over, I'd put a propane stove in my yurt."

RADIANT HEAT

Radiant heat, also called hydronics (a system that runs hot water in pipes through the floor), is the most efficient and comfortable form of heating for any shelter. Christian Bartsch, who made a radiant cob floor for his yurt, points out that the biggest challenge in heating yurts is the way that localized heat gets funneled up and out of the skylight bubble before it heats up the rest of the room. This makes floor heat an ideal option for yurts because the entire yurt is evenly warmed as the heat rises from the floor.

A typical hydronics floor of poured concrete (or cob or adobe) may be too permanent for the transitional nature of many fabric yurt applications. There are, however, systems available that use a less permanent framed floor; the Warmboard brand is one example. Options for heating the water (if you don't have a hot springs nearby) include a wood or propane-fired boiler, a wood-stove, or electricity.

Pete Dolan of Pacific Yurts shared this example of a yurt with a wooden radiant floor: "We had a customer who designed a rectangular structure with a roof built of SIPs rated at around R-30. On top of this structure he laid the two-by-six joists for his circular yurt platform and had the water tubes snake between the joists. He then laid plywood flooring over the joists. A propane-fired hot-water heater in the rectangular structure below supplied the hot water for the radiant heat."

ELECTRIC HEAT

Electric heat is used in some yurts in the form of baseboard heating or electrically heated radiators. If you have inexpensive electrical power, electric heat is certainly an option. The new electric ceramic heaters are rated well for efficiency and are worth checking into. You may find, though, that electric heat, being the least efficient of all the options, serves you best as a supplement to other forms of heating.

The felted covering of the Central Asian ger makes it perfectly suited for the extremely cold but dry conditions of the high Asian steppes. Felt doesn't work well in the damper climates of Europe and North America; some form of canvas or architectural fabric is used instead. Since canvas and most architectural fabrics don't have any natural insulative qualities, some type of insulation must be added.

The insulation most commonly used by yurt companies consists of one or two layers of plastic bubble wrap sandwiched between two layers of reflective foil (technically called Radiant Barrier Foil, RBF). The foil works by reflecting radiant heat in both directions (inside for winter and outside for summer), making this a lightweight but highly effective form of insulation.

The reflective insulation used in yurts was developed by NASA and is more effective than most other forms of insulation. Over 75 percent of a building's heat loss or gain is through radiation. Conventional mass insulation products like fiberglass or loose-fill insulation have very little effect on radiant heat loss (reducing it by 5 to 10 percent), but RBF reduces radiant heat transfer by as much as 97 percent.

Unlike mass insulation, adding multiple layers of reflective insulation provides little added benefit—especially relative to the additional cost. It may be more cost effective to add some of the custom options offered by yurt companies, like window insulation or a dome insulation panel (which will keep the heat from going out of your skylight bubble and create tensional airflow to circulate the heat back down).

You might save money by providing your own insulation. On my last yurt, I purchased only the ceiling insulation package from the company and went online to order bubble wrap and commercial-strength RBF. I taped the layers of bubble wrap and foil together with duct tape (spray adhesive would have worked as well) and pinned them to the inside of the trellis wall. To cover the insulation, I purchased enough muslin for my entire inside wall, had it hemmed into wall-length curtains, and hung it from the tension cable over the insulative material. This created an attractive interior (covering most of the crosshatching of the trellis wall) and had the additional advantage of allowing extra airspace around the reflective material. If you insulate in this manner, be sure to put a reflective layer on the outside of the bubble wrap as well as the inside to reflect heat away from the yurt in the summer.

The Alaskan company Nomad Shelter has developed a three-tiered insulation system. They recommend the standard insulation package with reflective foil and bubble wrap for yurts used only in the summer months. For year-round Alaska living, they sell a heavier insulation package that adds a layer of hollow fiber batting with a backing of Tyvek building wrap. This layer is attached outside of the reflective insulation (the reflective insulation layer provides an inner vapor barrier for the fiber batting). If more insulation is required, they suggest adding a third layer of one-inch rigid foam insulation.[12]

Any yurt owner can add these layers, using fiber-fill batting (the kind used for quilting) or synthetic felt, with a vapor barrier to keep the batting or felt from collecting condensation. Like the Asian nomads, you can also hang decorative rugs and quilts on your walls, thereby adding more internal layers of insulation as well as decoration. To insulate my windows, I use heavy theater curtains that I found in a recycling shop. I had them re-hemmed to cover the entire window panels from floor to ceiling, and then I hung them from the tension cable. They've worked well. Remember that home-built insulation won't always contain fire retardant, so be careful of fire danger when doing the insulating yourself.

Insulating the floor is also important. You can place conventional types of mass insulation under the floor (as in a traditional house) or use SIPs (with built-in insulation) to build the deck as explained earlier. Remember to use reflective insulation as well as conductive insulation under the floor.

I insulated underneath my yurt platform with two layers of rigid foam insulation. I placed the top layer an inch and a half under the plywood floor, with the reflective coating face up (a reflective layer works best with an inch of air space in front of it). I attached another thicker layer of rigid foam under the two-by-six-inch joists. This system combines two insulating air sections with the two layers of rigid foam and one reflective layer for maximum insulating effect.

You might also want to add skirting around the bottom of the platform. I use straw bales under my platform on the windward side. In the spring, the straw can be used as mulch in the garden.

What you put on top of your floor is also important. Carpet can function as an extra layer of insulation. In the summer, I use grass mats to keep my floor feeling cool, and in the winter I change to nice wooly rugs for added warmth.

Finally, an additional layer of winter insulation can be added to the ceiling using rigid foam. The foam is cut into triangles to fit between the rafters (with the reflective side of the foam facing in). Some of the yurt companies include measurements for the insulation triangle with their set-up plans.

Regardless of what you do to heat and insulate, the temperature in a yurt will still be more variable than in a site-built wooden or earthen home. One final option is to learn from cultures without central heating.

My mother tells a story about working as an American teacher in a coastal town in Brittany, France. There was no central heat in her quarters, and she was allowed only enough wood to heat her stone-cold room for one hour each day. She believes she would have died from prolonged hypothermia if she hadn't discovered a secret. Her colleagues, all fashionable Frenchwomen, were wearing woolen underwear. My mother followed suit and her problem was solved. What's the moral of her story? Don't just heat the air in your surroundings; insulate yourself as well! Put on a sweater, wear layers, and enjoy fuzzy socks and felted slippers.

One of my favorite nighttime tricks is to use hot-water bottles, a British custom. If you put a couple of them in your bed while you're brushing your teeth, you'll be amazed at how luxuriously warm your bed will feel by the time you slide in. Hot-water bottles can help you stay warm through the night, when your thermostat is turned down or if the fire in your woodstove goes out.

Keeping Cool

Yurts can be an ideal shelter for tropical climates, where heating needs are minimal and most cooling needs can be met with proper siting and adequate ventilation.

The Central Asian nomads roll up the felt along the bottom of their yurts to create cross ventilation during hot spells, and they use reed screens instead of felt as wall coverings in the warmer southern areas. It's possible to roll up the sides on a fabric yurt and hang mosquito netting along the lattice wall, although most modern yurts aren't designed to facilitate this. Other methods are more commonly used for creating cross ventilation.

You probably will want to have extra screened windows as part of your yurt package, including one across from your door, for cross ventilation. Most of the yurt companies have versions of screen doors or screen curtains for the front door. Colorado Yurt Company has optional wall sections that are screened top to bottom (see photo below).

Fans are as helpful for circulating cool air in the summer as they are for circulating hot air in the winter. Pacific Yurts also suggests putting vents in the floor to make use of cool air under the yurt.

The insulation you get with your yurt will have reflective foil inside and out. As previously explained, the purpose of the outer reflective layer is to reflect summer heat away from the yurt. This will make a huge difference in keeping your yurt cool.

It's amazing how much heat is caused by the sun coming in through the skylight. I can see the path the sun has taken around my yurt on a hot summer day by where my candles have melted. Some of the yurt companies sell tinted skylight

Some yurt companies have conversion kits to turn their window covers into awnings, providing protection from both sun and rain.

bubbles and shade screens that can be placed in the center ring. If you have a climate like mine that has cold winters and hot summers, the removable shade screen is a great idea for the summer. If you have a skylight bubble, a dome opener is essential for ventilation. Pacific Yurts also sells a raised cupola, a steel frame with a fabric cover that replaces the skylight bubble and creates a natural cooling system for tropical climates.

Conversion kits can turn your window covers into awnings. This provides protection from the sun, and you will be able to leave your windows open without worrying about a summer rainstorm while you're gone.

Some yurt owners in the southwestern United States install evaporative (swamp) coolers for air-conditioning, using an extra door frame to hold the air conditioner. Air-conditioning units have

Colorado Yurt Company offers an optional screened-wall section to provide ventilation. Two adjacent screened panels can give the feeling of a screened-in porch.

also been installed in rental campground yurts in Canada.

yurt utilities

If you are in a rural location, you might want to consider alternatives to conventional utilities. Information on sawdust and composting toilets, solar power, and propane appliances can be found in the Resource Guide under "Homesteading and Sustainable Living."

Electricity and plumbing can be brought up through the floor or through interior partition walls in the yurt. As in a conventional home, the most efficient design places bathroom and kitchen so that utilities for both can be brought up through the same wall. You can do almost anything in a yurt with utilities that you can do in a conventional home.

MAKING A YURT

If you have carpentry and sewing skills and want the experience of creating your own shelter, then by all means order a set of plans (see the Resource Guide under "Plans") and go for it. For this project, you'll need a commercial sewing machine (which can be rented), woodworking tools, and a workshop space. Keep in mind that some of the plans available online are camping yurt designs and may not be appropriate for year-round living.

Making a yurt requires the same care and attention to detail that building a house does. A friend of mine who has made three yurts warns that the process can be stressful. Keep in mind when making your decision that the markup on commercially produced fabric yurts isn't high; if you buy from a reputable company, you will get an excellent value for your investment and your home will be up in a matter of days.

There are three major yurt companies in the United States: Pacific Yurts in Cottage Grove, Oregon; Colorado Yurt Company in Montrose, Colorado; and Rainier Yurts (formerly Nesting Bird Yurts) in Seattle, Washington. Colorado Yurt Company has a German subsidiary (Advance Canvas), and Rainier Yurts kept the Nesting Bird name for their French company. Yurtco in Burnaby, British Columbia, is Canada's largest company.

These companies have been around a number of years, they've successfully placed yurts in state and provincial parks, they have experience with building code issues, and they also have reputations

This yurt frame was hand built by Society of Creative Anachronism (SCA) enthusiast Bill Lubarsky, who conceived his plans from pictures in sources like *National Geographic*. "I wanted something I could carry and set up myself," he says. The frame is built from two-by-four stock, and solid oak boards were steamed and bent to create the center ring, or crown.

It's important to take as much care in choosing a yurt company as you do in choosing the yurt design itself.

Beware of companies that make extravagant claims, like having the best or strongest yurts at the lowest price. You usually get what you pay for with a yurt. Also, don't judge a company solely on its Web site. If you have questions about a yurt company, ask for references and check with the local Better Business Bureau. See if the company has yurts near you that you can visit or if they are going to be at an upcoming trade show that you can attend.

Here are some questions to ask a company's references:

- Was your yurt delivered on time?
- Was everything included in the yurt kit when it arrived?
- Were there hidden costs you weren't told about initially?
- How easy was your yurt to put up? How helpful were the written set-up instructions and deck plans?
- What kind of customer-service support did the company offer?
- Are you pleased with the design and quality of your yurt? Have you experienced any problems?

for strong designs and excellent customer support. Each company has also, over the years, developed optional items (in response to customer requests) that can be custom ordered to solve various problems or make a yurt more comfortable.

There are smaller companies that have also been around for years making simple, pleasant yurts for regional and custom markets. Nomad Shelter is a family business that sells primarily to the Alaskan market (see their story on page 98). Kirk Bachman in Stanley, Idaho, continues to specialize in rustic-style backcountry yurts. There are also companies that make camping-style yurts primarily for Society of Creative Anachronism (SCA) reenactment events. New yurt businesses appear often and may have the lowest price because their overhead is lower. They are also more likely to produce the more rustic-style yurts. However, the buyer may not

get the experience, expertise, and engineering back-up that are a part of purchasing from an established company. Newer companies are also less likely to have all the custom options that the larger companies do.[13]

The real issue in buying a yurt is to determine what your priorities are and find the company that meets your needs most effectively. Here are some other things to keep in mind:

Customer service is especially important with a yurt because, regardless of the seeming simplicity of yurts, [1] you've probably never lived in one before, [2] you've probably never set one up before, and [3] yurt designs vary from one company to another. It's important to be able to go to the source for answers. When you walk into your local hardware store with questions about your yurt, they may look at you blankly, like you just got off a spaceship from

Mars. That's why it's great to have a yurt company customer-service representative just a phone call away who has seen your problem dozens–if not hundreds–of times and has answers and options ready for you. Since companies' designs are different, many parts are not interchangeable. Keep in mind when shopping for yurts that the company you buy from now is probably the one you're going to be dealing with for many years. Make sure you're comfortable with them and that you like their design.

Remember, too, that you want your yurt company to be around when you need to purchase replacement parts in two years, add awnings in five years, or get a new wall or roof cover in ten or fifteen years. Selling yurts is a challenging business, and yurt companies come and go. If you want to be in your yurt long term, make sure you're buying from a company that is likely to be there for you down the road.

custom options

Be sure when you are shopping for yurts that you explore the custom options that each company offers. There are some wonderful possibilities, like French doors, water-catchment systems, prefabricated platforms and window-awning conversion kits. Be aware that what are custom add-on items for one company may be part of another's package.

There are some options that should be included in almost all yurt applications. Unless you are buying an over-the-door front awning with your yurt, you should, for instance, get a rain diverter (sometimes called a "cricket"). Even a covered porch is difficult to attach in such a way that rain is diverted from the front door. On a rainy day, the rain diverter will keep you from getting soaked as you enter the yurt, and it will prevent water damage to your door frame.

Another option worth serious consideration is the skylight dome opener, both for added ventilation in the summer and for winter ventilation in case your woodstove gets smoky. Some kind of screen door or screen curtain for each door is also helpful in any climate.

SETTING UP A YURT

It can take from a few days to a couple of weeks to build your deck platform, depending on your carpentry skills, the site, and weather conditions (see Appendix 2 for a sample platform diagram). If you're not skilled in carpentry, you may want to hire professionals to build the platform or a carpenter to work with you as lead on the project.

The rain diverter, or "cricket" (shown above the door), and a screen door or curtain should be included in most yurt purchases.

A backyard yurt provided a unique solution for Joe and Barb Boud, a California couple, who had a typical teenager "problem." "As our boys grew into teenagers, so did their friends," says Joe. "We found our house full of what had been small people—now big people—and with their growing independence came their loud music, boisterous games, computers and printers, deep voices, and stinky feet. Barb and I knew it was time to reclaim our home, though we do love having all these wonderful kids around."

Barb and Joe considered building a permanent recreation room in the backyard, but the combination of permit fees and construction costs made it cost prohibitive. Joe knew about yurts from architecture school, so they ordered a yurt. Building the deck and erecting the yurt became a family project, with the boys taking ownership from the start.

One family's solution to the conflict of sharing space with growing teenagers and their friends was to move the teens to their own space in the backyard. Father and sons built a deck and erected the yurt together, with help from the boys' friends. "Once it was finished," says Joe Boud, "my wife, Barb, and I found ourselves frequently hanging out in the yurt. It is such a warm and inviting living space. Now, it was the two of us that were asked to leave! And when our boys grow up and fly off on their own, we can dismantle the yurt and move it up to our coastal ranch property."

Before setting up the yurt, it is helpful to read over the instructions to make sure you understand everything. If something doesn't make sense, call the yurt company. Have them fax you a picture if necessary. On one of my yurts, the orientation of the rafters was described but no picture was supplied (the company has since rewritten the instructions with pictures for every step). Three of us thought from the description that the rafters should go one way; one person thought the reverse. Majority ruled, and to this day (I'm embarrassed to say) my rafters are upside down.

An average-sized yurt takes less than one day to put up; a thirty-foot yurt can take two days. It's a good idea to have help, preferably three or more people. The single most important factor in a successful yurt raising is to follow the instructions exactly. It helps to have one designated person read the instructions out loud step-by-step as other people do the work. I remember one instance in a yurt raising when three people had to come back and spend an hour fixing what someone had jumped ahead to do because "it seemed obvious."

Some yurt companies recommend renting scaffolding to put up the center ring. It's also possible to rent a Genie lift or use a beam lifter (with extensions added) to raise the ring to the correct height. These options are essential for setting the heavier rings of large yurts (twenty-four-foot and thirty-foot), and may be helpful for smaller yurts as well. It is possible on the smaller yurts to have three or four people raise the ring using rafters, as the Turkic tribes do.

When raising the ring with rafters, be sure to mark both the center ring and the tension cable (using masking tape) with the placement for your first three or four rafters at equidistant intervals (check the diagrams in your plans to get the spacing right). Have everyone clear the platform except for those raising the ring, and make sure that all children stay clear until all the rafters are placed. Slip two rafters into the ring where marked and lift the ring off the ground, letting the legs of the two rafters support it. Insert the third rafter and use it to hoist the center ring into position. Keeping pressure against the first two rafters, place the notched end of the third rafter on the cable. Place the other two rafters at their positions on the cable, and then begin adding the remaining rafters in a symmetrical pattern (one rafter, then a rafter opposite it, and then the third leg of the triangle). It may help while raising the ring to have a fourth person use a rafter to balance the ring as it is moved into position. Wear hard hats, take your time, and be careful.

MAINTAINING A YURT

The wooden framework of a yurt is built to last indefinitely. The fabric covering is supposed to last from five years (for the walls) to ten or fifteen years (for the roof), after which time it may need to be replaced. Often the coverings last much longer, though this is dependent on weather conditions and siting. Lots of sun exposure will break down the material more quickly, and a lot of rain at a forest site may lead to mold problems and disintegration. When buying a used yurt, it's important to find out how old the fabric parts are, as you may incur a major expense if you have to promptly replace them.

In wet climates, it's a good idea to scrub canvas

(or cotton-containing) walls once or twice a year with a biodegradable fungicide. In a climate with a lot of sun exposure, some yurt owners paint the outside of their older canvas walls to make them last a year or two longer (however, this affects the breathe-ability of the fabric). If you have a yurt with moveable wall panels, you can move the panels around to extend their life. When cleaning modern architectural fabrics, it is important to follow the directions that come with your yurt. Household chemical cleaners can ruin architectural fabrics. Some companies recommend a mild detergent soap while others recommend special soaps created by the fabric manufacturers.

Any exterior wood (like the door frame) may need to be recoated with a wood finish every couple of years. Your yurt company will tell you if this is necessary. If so, they can recommend finishes.

BATHROOMS AND KITCHENS

The location of bathrooms is a matter of personal choice. Many people prefer to keep their toilet and shower outside of the yurt (for example, in a separate bathhouse outbuilding) or to use an outhouse with a composting or sawdust bucket toilet.[14] It's common to build a small wood-framed structure for this purpose. You could also purchase a small matching yurt or build a small tapered wall outhouse yurt.

If bathroom and kitchen facilities are located inside the yurt, plumbing can be brought up through the yurt floor, while the yurt platform is being built.

In a cold climate where pipes can freeze, some people build a separate framed-in structure that can be well insulated, and then provide a thermostat-controlled heat source like a vented propane heater. Putting all the plumbing in an outbuilding gives the

Many yurt owners build a bathhouse adjacent to their yurt, like the one on the right, which also has an outdoor shower. A separate bathhouse provides privacy, resolves plumbing issues, and makes more space available in the yurt. In cold climates an outbuilding can provide a well-insulated space for kitchen and bathroom with constant, thermostat-controlled heat to keep plumbing from freezing.

yurt owner the flexibility to leave for extended periods of time without having to heat the whole yurt.

Interior partition walls are built after the yurt has been erected and should be freestanding (not attached to the yurt framework). Electrical and plumbing work (usually shared by an adjoining bathroom and kitchen) can be installed in the partition walls, as they would in any house. For more information and floor plans, see the last chapter, "Living in the Round."

FINANCING AND INSURANCE

Yurt companies do not offer financing. Usually they ask for half of the contracted price down before they begin making your yurt. You pay the other half when you pick up the yurt or have it shipped.

Individuals may get a personal loan or line of credit from their bank or utilize a credit card for their yurt purchase. Commercial enterprises like resorts or campgrounds can finance yurts on a lease or loan basis through a business finance company (two are listed under "Yurt Companies" in the Resource Guide).

Mortgage bankers normally will not loan money to finance a yurt home for the same reason they won't finance trailers on wheels. If you move your yurt and don't pay the lender, they are left with nothing that can be held as "surety." Standard construction loans apply only to a constructed house, manufactured home, or trailer that is tied in to a foundation. Insurance companies, likewise, will not insure fabric yurts unless they are added to a policy that includes a constructed building as a primary residence or workplace.

In some ways, borrowing for a yurt is like borrowing to purchase a car. The price tag is similar and both can be moved. However, with a vehicle there is a title issued by the state that the lender will hold on to until you've paid in full. There is no title for a yurt and no state involvement, so, again, a lender has no way of insuring itself against loss.

It may be possible to purchase a piece of property and then, after a period of time, request an equity loan to cover the cost of your yurt (your loan officer can tell you if you need a "seasoning" period between when you purchase the land and when you can pull equity out of it). Variables affecting the lender's response include how quickly the market value of property is going up in your area, the terms of your loan (i.e., the number of years), and how much money you have down.

If you want to fully explore financing possibilities, establish a relationship with a loan officer early in the process. Explain that you want to purchase a "nonconforming home" (i.e., not stick-built, manufactured, or HUD-labeled). It will help if you can bring in information; pictures, especially, will serve to illustrate exactly what you are talking about. Let the person leaf through this book and leave a full-color brochure from your yurt company with him or her.

We're accustomed to thinking in terms of financing an entire house project at once. However, if financing is difficult to obtain, the flexible nature of the fabric yurt allows you to create a home space in stages as finances become available. You can purchase the shell of the yurt and the basics first and live with fewer amenities until you can afford them. Options like plumbing, power, and phone lines can be added at a later date (this will be easier with a little advance planning). At least you'll have a lovely space to live in rent free while you save for the rest.

BUILDING CODES

One of the most complicated issues people face when wanting to use a yurt as either a home or workspace involves the building permit process. Code requirements vary from state to state and within counties and local communities. Individual officials, even within the same locale, may interpret the rules differently. Add to this the fact that many code officials have little or no experience with yurts, and you have a situation that can become very confusing.

Before you buy a yurt, it's a good idea to check with your local planning and zoning office to see what the rules are in your area and how local officials are likely to respond to your particular yurt application. Here are some questions to get you started:

o— Which set of code regulations is this department using? They will probably tell you either the UBC (Uniform Building Code, US) or the ICC codes (International Code Council, US and international).[15]

o— Has the department previously approved yurts in this city or county? If so, which manufacturers have been approved?

o— Is a yurt considered to be an "alternative structure"?

o— What are the specific requirements in this area for snow load, seismic rating, and wind speed? Are there any other special requirements?

o— What are their fire-rating requirements for the insulation and outer fabric?

o— If the planning and zoning office hasn't previously worked with yurts (or with your prospective company), is there a state-certified engineer to whom your yurt company can send engineering specs for review? (The engineering specifications must relate to the strength and stability of the yurt as a complete assembly, not just component parts.)

o— Would the planning office find it helpful to have contact information for building officials in other places where your company's yurts have been approved?

Here are some things to keep in mind as you go through the permitting process:

As a membrane structure, yurts are usually classified in the "alternative structures" category, which has a unique set of code regulations. (In Appendix 1, you'll find excerpts from the 2003 IBC Alternative Structures section.) If your yurt is classified as a permanent or long-term alternative structure, it will have to meet local requirements for snow load, wind speed, and seismic ratings. You will also have to show that the yurt materials are fire retardant. If your yurt is being set up as a temporary structure for six months or less, the requirements are much more flexible.

Local stipulations vary. For example, a town might have a snow-load requirement of twenty-five pounds per square foot, and nearby ski resort could have a requirement of one hundred pounds per square foot. When you talk with your yurt company, you might find out that their standard snow-and-wind kit would work for the in-town requirement, but for the ski resort you would need to purchase a yurt that has been specifically engineered for heavier snow loads.

If your yurt will be used for residential purposes, it will also have to meet local regulations for residences (like heat source, egress windows in sleeping areas, and so on). If you are using the yurt for commercial purposes, you'll have to meet an additional set of commercial regulations.

The biggest code challenge for yurts is insulation. Building codes rate insulation by R-value alone. R-value (resistance to conductive heat transfer) analyzes only conductive or mass-type insulation; it has no category or parameters for reflective insulation. As described earlier, reflective insulation is far more efficient than conductive.[16] However, for the purposes of current building codes, reflective insulation does not exist. The type of reflective insulation used in yurts can be rated only in conductive terms, which in the case of a layer or two of bubble wrap (the conductive element) gives a very low rating.

Your code official may understand the efficacy of your reflective insulation and be willing to figure in other factors, like your heat source.[17] It may be possible to get an exemption from the energy code if you are incorporating a renewable heat source or if the yurt is not being heated continuously (such as when occupancy is "transient and intermittent," as with camping rentals or vacation retreats).[18]

However, if your official feels compelled to stay within code parameters and your yurt is a permanent residence, it may be difficult to get your yurt approved. This is the time to provide your code official with the contact information for other code officials who have yurt experience and can point out ways to get around the apparent difficulties. Certainly, if yurts have been approved for resorts and parks from South Carolina to Alaska and for uses as diverse as schools and offices as well as residences, a well-engineered yurt should have strong potential for approval in most locales.

At Mt. Orford Ski Resort in Quebec, Canada, three yurts are joined together with covered walkways between them. The lashing on the outside of the yurts and the center brace are parts of Pacific Yurts snow-and-wind kit, added to meet snow-load and wind requirements at the ski resort.

BOTTOM RIGHT: Rainier Yurts has developed a system using blocks placed between rafters to keep them from twisting, which allows for an increased snow-load capacity of 50 to 90 percent.

Some yurt companies started as family businesses and have kept their family feel through the years. For Jessica and Lee Tenhoff in Alaska, and Dan and Emma Kiger in Colorado, making yurts is a labor of love and a family affair. Here are their stories.

NOMAD SHELTER YURTS

"Lee and I made our first yurt in 1987," explains Jessica Tenhoff. "I had just given birth to our firstborn. It was January in Fairbanks, Alaska, and we lived in a cabin a half mile off the road. Lee pulled us home on a sled after my thirty-six-hour labor at a birthing center. He tucked me and Zeke into the cabin and then went out to get propane. While he was away, the entire second floor caught fire and the cabin was fully engulfed when I woke up. We lost everything except the baby and the clothes we had on.

"Lee was in flight school at the time and not working, so friends threw us a fundraiser. We spent $250 on canvas and hardware to build the yurt. Lee cut spruce poles and lashed the joints, doing everything with hand tools. We moved into the yurt with the baby in a little over a month.

"That was our first yurt and we traveled with it everywhere. We took it to Valdez for a year and shipped it to the beach at Nome, Alaska, to look for gold for a season. Moving in our yurt turned out to be a great way to try out places before sinking roots.

"Wherever we went, people were interested in the yurt, so one winter when there were no jobs, we took out a free classified ad in the *Homer Tribune* to see if there was local interest in buying yurts. We got lots of calls and the newspaper did a story on us, so we took out a loan for a sewing machine and materials for our first order, and Nomad Shelter Yurt Company was born. That was 1995, and we've been making yurts commercially in Alaska ever since.

"Our customers find us mainly by word of mouth. About 90 percent of them are single professional women—teachers, massage therapists, and so on—using our yurts as primary residences in Alaska. Go figure. We thought outfitters, camps, and macho-expedition, outdoorsy types would go for the yurts, but that's not who buys them. Guys up here know they can make a plywood shack themselves more cheaply, I guess. Women don't want plywood shacks, and they want the interiors to look finished. Plus, you don't have to be a long-term carpenter to set up a yurt.

"Our Alaskan customers seem to really 'get it' about simplified living and elegant, low-impact, sustainable lifestyles. We meet some great people in this business, and we feel good about what we make. I guess those are the things that make the business work for us."

COLORADO YURT COMPANY

"I met Emma back in the early seventies," explains Dan Kiger. "I was fresh out of a too-academic college career studying Irish poets and French painters, and I was hankering for a real job—one that involved tools and handiwork. I was living in an old miner's cabin eleven thousand feet up a Colorado mountainside, and Emma was the only one higher than I—a good thousand feet higher, in a field of wildflowers. Before long we built a tipi and set up housekeeping together along the path between our two cabins. Our first tipi was built to last—a philosophy we've maintained ever since.

"It was a mile trek from the road to the tipi so we got plenty of skiing in that first winter. Heavier loads were handled by our sled dogs. We both enjoyed the benefits of living in the woods, but Emma felt drawn back to the University of Michigan. So I brought the tipi back to Michigan and set it up on a farm where we lived while Emma finished her degree. Our first tipi stayed in Michigan as a donation to an alternative high school where Emma was teaching science.

"Our second tipi was built in the halls of U of M after graduation. Imagine our surprise when we hauled it out to the center of campus at midnight to scribe and fold it and the sprinkler system came on. What do you do with a thousand square feet of soaking wet canvas? Throw it in the back of the truck and head west. Three days later the tipi was dried out and pitched once again on our Colorado mountainside.

"When word got around the community that we had made our own tipi, we had a dozen tipis to make and our business was born. We set up shop in an old barn, emptied the savings account to pay for a couple of industrial sewing machines and set to work.

"The design elements of our tents, tipis, and, in 1983, yurts came from some of the great books that still sit on our shelves: *Shelter, The Indian Tipi,*

The Whole Earth Catalog, and *The Owner-Built Home,* to name a few. We got our mail-order business rolling the old-fashioned way–with print advertising in publications like the *Mother Earth News* and *East-West Journal.* Orders literally came through the mail and it was a thrill to correspond with and sometimes meet our customers from all over the country.

"It's still a thrill. We now have customers from all over the world. We were especially honored when a Ute elder toured our display yurt, pronounced the structure worthy of use in ceremonies, and placed an order for his own yurt.

"We've tried to stick with the same principles we started with. Our shop is partially solar heated, our office yurt is off the grid, and we run bio-diesel in our trucks. Today the Colorado Yurt Company occupies a small campus of buildings where twenty-five highly motivated people come to work every day. What hasn't changed for us is the importance of craftsmanship and innovation and the values of enduring partnerships, reliability, and know-how."

An early yurt, built by Jessica and Lee Tenhoff of Nomad Shelter Yurts, stands silhouetted against a display of northern lights. The Lexan panel skylight with the stovepipe coming up through the middle is typical of these classic-style Alaska yurts.

THE FRAME PANEL YURT

"'There can be no power in a square,' Black Elk said. 'You will notice that everything an Indian does is in a circle, and that is because the power of the world always works in circles, and everything tries to be round.' . . . Nature creates in circles and moves in circles. Atoms and galaxies are circular, and most organic things in between. The earth is round. The wind whirls. The womb is no shoebox. Where are the corners of the egg and the sky?"

—Tom Robbins, *Even Cowgirls Get the Blues*

In 1985, Richard and Priscilla Comen decided to take an early retirement and move to land they had purchased in lovely Mendocino County, California. At a home show in San Francisco, they came across David Raitt and his company, California Yurts.

"We liked the concept of a round structure," says Richard. "It would give us 360-degree views of our redwood-studded surroundings from each room, and the yurt design solved some of the challenges of our sloping piece of land. By raising the yurt off the ground on multiple pilings, and constructing it on multiple levels, we could avoid recontouring the land and removing extra redwood trees. The piling system would also anchor the yurt against the heavy rains that occur during the Mendocino winter season."

"We also realized that we could have a custom home without incurring high architectural fees because California Yurts had a group of existing plans that we could combine to accommodate our site needs, rather than starting from a blank sheet of paper."

The top photo shows the twenty-four-foot master bedroom suite of the Germani residence (see also pages 112–13). A low wall behind the bed shields the dressing area from the main space but allows light from the skylight to bathe the space. In the bottom photo, the Comens' home is set in a redwood forest. Like the Germani residence, it consists of two multistory yurts attached by a spacious passageway with additional rooms.

The flexible yurt is cozy and comfortable for the couple who lives here but also has accommodated up to sixty guests without feeling crowded.

"Another factor influencing our choice," Richard continues, "was the fact that the yurt was constructed off-site and arrived in sections by truck. It would be assembled on-site in a matter of days. This meant that the house could be livable within a very short time compared to conventional construction. Our yurt contractor also was amenable to the owners doing whatever our expertise would allow, and I was capable of doing the electrical, plumbing, and interior finish work myself."

"We built the house in 1986. We were very involved in the planning stage, and the whole process happened rapidly and easily. Now, twenty years later, we would do the same thing again. We have loved our home all these years."

"For those contemplating yurt construction," says Richard, "our main piece of advice would be to utilize the circle concept to its fullest and enjoy the open space; don't place partitions. If you want partitions, you might as well build a conventional square-room house."

The daytime living area in the thirty-one-foot yurt includes a living room, dining room, and kitchen. No space is wasted on partitions between rooms as in a conventional house.

The Comens' children are grown and living their own lives. "It is now just the two of us," says Richard, "and we are very pleased with our yurt home. It is easy to maintain, easy to clean, and is all on one level, which becomes important in one's older years."

The Comens' son Craig purchased land close to his parents in Fort Bragg, California. Planning to design a dream home with a magnificent ocean view, he started working with an architect. Gradually he realized how much the project would cost and that his vision might not be a good fit for his site. Craig had been visiting his parents in their yurt home for many years and had always loved the spacious feel of the yurts, their intimate connection to their surroundings, and their flexibility.

Craig met with David Raitt, his parents' designer, and came away with models that he could cut and paste into his own custom design. He decided on the Nautilus, a design based on the shape of a spiral, with two smaller rooms extending off of a twenty-six-foot great room. This fit Craig's budget, but he wanted more space so David added a loft to the design, covering half the great room and giving him a total of eleven hundred square feet.

The Comens have worked in the antiques business, and some of their favorite antiques grace this light-filled kitchen area.

California Yurts put up the basic structure of Craig Comen's yurt. Craig finished it, with help from his father and surfing buddies.

Craig Comen's father, Richard, designed and built this spiral staircase. The lighting fixtures were made by a friend. "Having California Yurts do everything wouldn't have been as enjoyable," says Craig. "Building it this way has made it a combination of many talents, with input from both my family and friends."

After two visits to California Yurts, Craig felt the design was ready to proceed. "I wanted to live in my house, not be a slave to it," says Craig, "so I kept it as simple as possible. I helped David's crew build the foundation and subfloor. Then a truck pulled in with the walls and we put them up in one day. David brought in a crane and we set all the roof panels on another day. The panels come with the interior already finished, so what was left for me to do was the exterior sheathing and trim and the interior finish work. Altogether it was a streamlined process, a real pleasure."

"I had the advantage of being able to rely on my dad's knowledge and his attention to detail. We worked together on the electrical, plumbing, and septic, and he taught me a lot. Members of my 'surfing brotherhood' also pitched in with lots of expertise in plumbing and other trades. We had a flexible work schedule. The understanding was 'if the surf is good, we'll go surfing.' My home is a combination of many talents, with lots of input from both family and friends."

Craig appreciated the overall process. "Calling it prefab isn't entirely accurate," he says. "It's really a custom home. The walls and roof panels are prefabricated. I enjoyed being able to finish it myself, despite some of the frustrations I experienced dealing with the odd angles of a circular structure."

"Interior decorating has been a challenge since most furniture is designed to fit into square spaces. My space is more of a challenge than my parents' place because it's smaller," says Craig. "Creativity and allowing it to evolve have been key."

Yurt-builder and designer David Raitt added extra floor space to Craig Comen's yurt by using tall walls and building in a loft.

FRAME PANEL YURTS:
CUSTOM PREFABRICATION

Many early frame panel customers were fabric yurt dwellers who wanted something more permanent. They were ready to settle down and take advantage of the comforts and amenities that a mortgage allows, but they didn't want to go back to living in boxes.

David Raitt of California Yurts, and Morgan Reiter of Oregon Yurtworks after him, devised a means of providing custom wooden yurts for clients at reasonable prices by using techniques of prefabrication.

Clients choose from a number of designs and make adjustments to fit their needs. "It's always been a client-driven business," says Morgan. "People come to us and say, 'I have this need; can you fill it?' It used to be a need for a small, affordable space. Today, it might be for a city hall, a medical building, or a small guest yurt out back. We truly do build everything 'from cabins to castles.'"

"By now we have done this enough," Morgan continues, "to really feel that the possibilities are endless and the design potential unlimited." Clients can also decide whether to have their yurt completed by a local contractor or do some of the work themselves, as the Comens did on their projects.

Like the two Comen projects, the yurt walls and roof are prefabricated into insulated, panelized sections. Fabrication happens in a shop, using volume production techniques that reduce waste and keep costs down. Once the on-site foundation is complete, the wall sections are trucked to the site and pieced together by a company crew, section by section. The roof, in triangular framed and pre-insulated panels, is also set by the crew, panel by panel. The entire process is fast, efficient, and produces minimal waste, all of which help make it cost effective for the client.

"I designed our modular system to use materials very efficiently, with four-foot-wide wall panels and triangular roof sections," Morgan explains. "If you compare one of our thousand-square-foot yurts with a conventional square building of the same size, our waste is 20 to 70 percent less than the square building. That's true in part because the conventional house is often a one-time building project and there's no thought given to efficiency of material. With modularization, one of the keys to success is to be efficient with your materials."

From large institutional buildings, like the Veneta City Hall in Oregon (two photos at left), to small, affordable living spaces, like this fabric artist's home (photo at right), frame panel yurts have been designed to meet a variety of needs.

DESIGN IN THE ROUND
INTERVIEW WITH MORGAN REITER

Morgan Reiter was exposed to Bill Coperthwaite's yurts while he was an architecture student in New England. There he also met David Raitt, a former student of Bill's who at the time was building tapered wall yurts. Morgan's interest was piqued, and he focused part of his academic work on an exploration of indigenous structures.

When Morgan moved west to a community in the Applegate Valley of Oregon, he decided to design and build his own shelter, synthesizing the yurt ideas he had seen in New England with indigenous concepts and his own design modifications. While building conventional structures as a business, Morgan started building yurts on the side for friends who saw his yurt and wanted one of their own. One yurt at a time, Oregon Yurtworks was born. Today it is the largest wooden yurt company in North America.

When did you first realize there was something special about yurts?
"Shortly after I started to build yurts as a business, we did a home show where we set up a demonstration

Architect Morgan Reiter, founder of Oregon Yurtworks, at work in his office, a tandem twenty-nine-foot and twenty-four-foot structure. The twenty-nine-foot yurt pictured has been divided so that there are two private offices to the left.

yurt. People would walk in, look around, and then comment on how good it felt. I remember a woman leaning over to her husband and saying, 'I love the way this feels!' It was the first time I'd ever seen a building produce an emotional reaction.

"When we'd do a home show with rectilinear models, people would make comments like 'love your work, nice lines' or 'nice trim work,' but we'd never get an emotional response. I realized that conventional construction can look nice, but with the yurt there is a 'feel,' an epiphany of sorts.

"It's been wonderful to design structures that can affect the way people feel. Our well-being, health, and attitudes are all affected by the spaces we live in. With a yurt, you're actually providing an experience that can enhance peoples' lives. A round building, instead of being a merely functional structure, is a beautiful, aesthetic, inviting, inspiring place to be."

You live and work in round buildings. What are some of the advantages of living and working in the round?

"Yurts are inspired. Rather than dreading going to a small, dark, constricted-feeling building, I look forward to spending my workdays in a light-filled, expansive space that is a pleasure to behold and a treat to work in. Yurts *do* add to one's day. They add a different interior environment.

"I also love living in a round building. After thirteen years, I still come home at night and look up at the circular ceiling and the beams and feel like they're welcoming me home, embracing me. The shape has always attracted me and worked for me–from an emotional and spiritual perspective. It's physical aspects are also appealing.

What do you find different about designing in the round?

"For me, the yurt is more of an art form than a construction form. When I'm designing a round building, I'm always thinking about how the outside interfaces with the inside and how the view interacts with the whole. This is because round buildings tend to be outwardly focused, rather than inwardly focused.

"We find that our clients also tend to be more outwardly focused. They care about the environment and their community; they want to interact with their surroundings. Their approach is, 'There's a whole world out there and I want to be part of it,' rather than, 'There's a whole world out there and I want to be shut off from it.'

"In our round buildings, we tend to place furniture in a more organic fashion, as in an inner space looking out. We find ourselves constantly drawing furniture into our designs, showing how the bed works better on an inner wall facing out or how the chairs are better clustered in the inside looking out rather than facing each other in a corner."

What attracts people to yurts?

"When I'm marketing a yurt, there are all of these hard facts that we present to people. Yurts are 10 to 20 percent less costly than comparable housing. They are more energy efficient (approximately 20 percent). The kit nature of the yurt allows the owner to be involved in the process of building in a barn-raising sense.

"Even though all of the above are true, these facts make a difference less than 10 percent of the time. People buy yurts because of how they feel, and all the rest is icing on the cake."

This sixty-four-foot concentric frame panel yurt houses the Applegate Medical Clinic. The upstairs contains a break room, storage rooms, and a doctor's office. The lower floor has a reception area, lab, nurses' station, business office, emergency room, x-ray room, two doctor's offices, and six exam rooms.

Are frame panel yurts portable?

"What we're doing with frame panel yurts is creating a kit, with pieces that are basically 'hand carry-able' but which we attach on-site in a way that is more permanent. The process of screwing the individual pieces together–or nailing, bolting, or cabling them–can be reversed.

"A chapel for three hundred people or a city hall is not a portable structure. However, the manner in which we build–with prefabricated components–does make portability an option. If someone says to us, 'I need a more formidable, secure, and insulated structure than the canvas yurt, but I'm not going to want it where it is forever,' we can make it work for them. It's important to note, however, that the systems–electrical, plumbing, and so on–do not move as easily, and that changes in building codes over time mean that what is legal this year may not be legal ten years down the line when the building is moved to another location."

The lower story of the Applegate Medical Clinic has a flat ceiling. This picture shows the lab, nurses' station, and hallways.

What's your advice regarding people building their own round structures?

"We don't really recommend building yourself because there's such a learning curve with round structures. While there's a plethora of instructional materials out there on square building that provides direction through every step of the process, this is not the case when building a conventional type of structure in the round. I'm afraid owner-builders won't get the quality they're looking for the first time around on a project, and it would be difficult to match in cost what we can do with our prefab modular approach.

"We've spent twenty years working with engineers, fabricators, and designers to make our yurts better and to ensure they meet the constantly changing building codes. I've spent over $100,000 on engineering alone over the years developing my designs, but I've spread it out over perhaps 500 yurts, so each owner isn't paying the real cost."

What has been your experience with codes and financing?

"We have never been turned down for a building permit to date. We tend to wow the building officials with fifty or more pages of engineering specs that have been developed, refined, and expanded over four hundred jobs and twenty years of building yurts. They realize we have done our homework and that these things just work.

"With bank officials we've found that the name *yurt* is more of a liability than an asset. So we

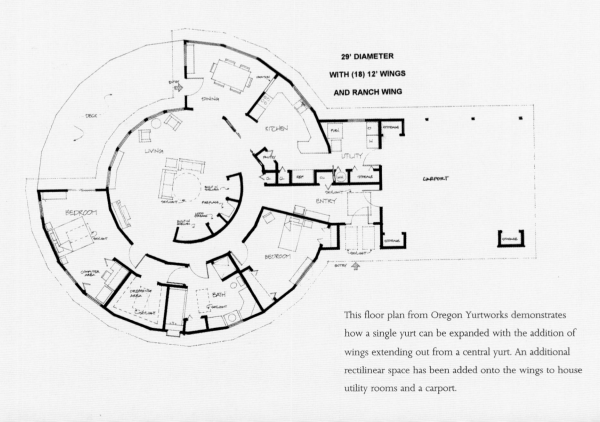

29' DIAMETER
WITH (18) 12' WINGS
AND RANCH WING

This floor plan from Oregon Yurtworks demonstrates how a single yurt can be expanded with the addition of wings extending out from a central yurt. An additional rectilinear space has been added onto the wings to house utility rooms and a carport.

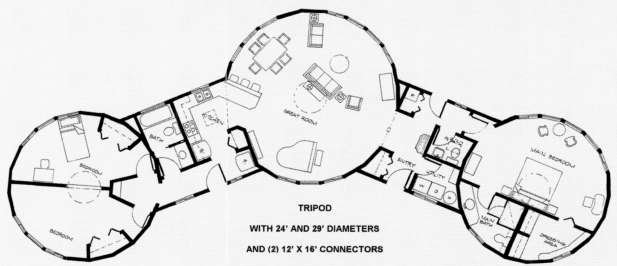

TRIPOD

WITH 24' AND 29' DIAMETERS

AND (2) 12' X 16' CONNECTORS

This floor plan uses multiple yurts with rectilinear connectors. Like the yurt on the back jacket of this book, the kitchen extends into a connector, making use of the rectilinear space to hang kitchen cabinets and incorporate appliances designed for square spaces.

describe our homes as 'architectural designed, custom round homes.' That nomenclature works better for officials who are conservative by nature."

Is living in the round for everyone?

"Round spaces are different. They are unique. They are enchanted. This reality, though, may not be for everyone.

"Some people are looking for a standardized perspective or for maximum efficiency. If you want an eight-by-ten-foot bedroom for a kid in which you can fit a bed and desk, you'll do best with a square shape. The furniture that's out there fits more efficiently and effectively into a square space than a round space, despite the fact that the round space actually feels more spacious."

What is so spectacular about yurts? What gives them that special feel?

"Part of the magic is the amount of light and energy that comes in through the skylight. When people walk into a yurt, their attention is drawn to the light at the center, and then their eyes pan back down and they look at this beautiful beam that runs down the ceiling. Rather than a dark castle, a protective shelter, it's an expansive structure. Round spaces tend to look and feel larger than square spaces, and the shape of the yurt makes it an uplifting, inspiring structure.

"Yurts are often placed in wooded settings and blend in naturally. In nature, you find irregular and curved shapes; there are no right angles. I find it jarring to come into a natural scene and see a house with sharp lines and jagged angles. When you walk into a beautiful, bucolic scene and see a yurt, its soft shape blends with its surroundings.

"There is a beauty, a wholeness, a magic to round buildings. I think humans have a natural affection for non-rectilinear shapes. It's simply more natural to build round rather than build a square building in a round world."

DESIGNING FOR RETIREMENT

For Jane and Paul Germani, building a prefab yurt was anything but a "cookie cutter" experience. The Germanis were not yet retirement age but wanted a home they could live in through their later years, which meant placing all the living spaces on one floor. Combining these design parameters with an already purchased hillside lot with lots of large trees that they wanted to keep made the design process complex. The Germanis took their time, though, and spent nine months working with Oregon Yurtworks to arrive at a design that fit both their aesthetic vision and their practical needs.

The Germanis' final design included a twenty-four-foot master bedroom yurt at street level, a large rectangular connecter (containing an entry hall, half bath, and kitchen) and a multistory twenty-nine-foot living room yurt at the back (the living room and kitchen are pictured on the back jacket of this book). A guest suite and artist's studio share the bottom floors of the hillside yurt tower and are connected to the living room by a winding staircase hung with art pieces.

Using the rectangular connector between the yurts allowed the Germanis to place kitchen cabinets into a traditional shape. "It gave us some wonderful and unexpected angles both in the kitchen and the master bath and added aesthetic interest to our house," says Jane.

"Take all the time you need to design the right house for your needs," Jane suggests. "Our long design process, which at the time seemed endless, turned out to be well worth it. Our yurt home is light and bright even on gray winter days. It is spacious and cozy, beautiful and aesthetically pleasing, and lends itself to casual, comfortable living. We have enjoyed living in our yurt home more than any house we have lived in over the course of thirty years."

FACING AND THIS PAGE: These photographs show different parts of the multistory twenty-nine-foot diameter yurt. Jane Germani's mosaic studio on the bottom floor (bottom right) includes a painted blue door inspired by a historical Italian crypt mosaic. The ceiling joists were left uncovered so that their design could be enjoyed. An art-filled hallway and staircase (bottom left) connect the art studio and a guest room on the lower floor with the living room on the main floor (top).

LA CASA BELLA
A SECOND HOME CLOSE TO HOME

Bob and Friedl Bell dreamed of building a second home "away from it all." For fifteen years, they looked at places like the Oregon coast, San Francisco, and even Italy, where their son and his family live. Finally they realized that the perfect setting might be right under their noses, in a forested lot adjacent to their property and only fifty feet from their home. "After seeing a yurt in the backyard of a house that was for sale," says Bob, "we began thinking that the setting of our side lot would be a perfect location for such a structure."

The Bells visited Oregon Yurtworks and shared their vision with Morgan Reiter. They wanted a special place for guests and family, where their sons could stay when visiting, with a platformed reading nook for the grandchildren. "Morgan had multiple suggestions," says Bob, "and presented us a plan reflecting our vision of the yurt's use." Because of neighborhood covenants, the yurt was designed as a "non-dwelling unit" with a full bathroom but without a full kitchen.

The Bells' advice for people furnishing a yurt is to keep it simple ("less is better") and to look for ways to save space. The Bells found a retractable screen door that takes up less space than an ordinary swinging door, and their thirty-gallon water heater is built into a cabinet that doubles as a counter with a butcher-block top. Friedl designed a bed using two single mattresses covered in boat-cushion material. The mattresses function as two twin beds or a single king and, when stacked against a wall with reclining cushions, double as a couch. "In a

The windowed back of the Bells' twenty-four-foot-diameter yurt looks out onto a forested hillside (photo on left). (The front of the yurt is shown on page 7.) This creative escape, although it contains only 454 square feet, easily accommodates an efficiency kitchen and full bath (photo at right).

With its many widows, this cozy living space feels connected to the forest around it. By not extending the dividing wall on the left to the ceiling, the architect allowed light from the skylight to flood into the kitchenette and bathroom behind the wall, giving them a light and airy feel.

yurt, the skylight and windows give the feeling of being outdoors," Bob points out, "so one should consider using colors and furnishings, which flow easily to the outside."

"Everything about the yurt has surpassed our expectations," Bob reflects. "We love its design, quality, and beauty. And what is it about a round house that is so radically different from a rectangular or square house with the same square footage? It

is remarkable. Our family and guests are reluctant to leave, and everyone who sees the yurt wants one."

When the Bells have no guests, they use the yurt for writing, playing jazz, and watching movies, or they watch deer and wild turkeys parade a safe distance from the yurt windows. "Sometimes we sit out there in the late afternoon with a glass of fine red wine and consider that life is pretty good."

LIVING IN THE ROUND

"There is something about the very shape of the circle that provides us a glimpse into the wholeness, unity, and divine order of the universe. The circle is a reflection of the world's—and our own—deep perfection, unity, design excellence, wholeness, and divine nature."

—Michael Schneider, *A Beginner's Guide to Constructing the Universe*

Paul and Criss Fosselman live in a thirty-foot fabric yurt with their "family" of two dogs and four cats. Paul, a web designer, works at home. Criss divides her time between an hourly job at a local health club and design work in quilts and fabric art.

Paul constantly thinks outside the box. For him the round, open space of their yurt is like a blank canvas that he and Criss can experiment with. "From an interior design perspective, the yurt is an open container," Paul says. "You can do anything you want with it. You can transform your space much more easily than in a standard box home, with its restrictions based on the architecture of the building. There, you're limited by the walls that exist and the way the spaces are defined by the building, which tells you, for example, that this room is a living room, that's a bedroom, and that one is a kitchen."

Paul's friends have commented that the yurt is arranged differently each time they visit. "When I lived in a box," says Paul, "I changed my stuff around a lot, but it wasn't the same. In a yurt, it's one big open space that can be defined at will, and we can determine how each space interacts with the other spaces. You could do that in a traditional home but you'd have to tear out walls and make major

Morgan Reiter of Oregon Yurtworks suggests to his frame panel yurt clients that they place their furniture in the center of the yurt, looking out. In Morgan's yurt home, the kitchen island and living room furnishings are placed to maximize the view and the connection between inside and outside.

construction changes. All we have to do is move our furniture around. The yurt allows us to create and re-create our space based on our current needs."

The openness of the yurt has also helped Paul and Criss move towards their goal of simplicity. "Because all of our possessions are with us in the yurt and visible at all times," says Paul, "we're much more aware of what's there and feel encouraged to sort more often. Our home encourages us to carefully consider what we acquire and give away what we don't need."

DEFINING SPACE WITHIN A YURT

As Paul and Criss found, yurt interiors are eminently flexible in their design. Fabric yurts in particular come without walls, rooms, or even closets. Even the permanent wooden yurts have fewer built-in components than their rectilinear counterparts.

There are two reasons for dividing up living spaces: to afford privacy and to provide functional separation for different activities. Thus comfortable

chairs adjacent to bookshelves can create a living room–a place to listen to music, read a book, or visit with friends. To peel potatoes, one moves to the kitchen, where the potatoes are stored close to a sink for washing and a peeler nestles in a drawer next to the sink. Functional separation helps us organize our spaces and keep our lives flowing smoothly.

In a yurt, privacy and functional separation can be achieved in a number of ways. Instead of rooms, many yurt dwellers use a combination of furniture placement, screens, bookshelves, and hanging fabric to define space and provide privacy.

If you want to keep the open feel of the yurt, you might choose to create visual divisions using furniture, rugs, and color differentiation. You might hang a translucent fabric or use a moveable screen to create privacy. Quite a few yurt dwellers hang curtains or fabric around the bed in an otherwise open-feeling yurt, thereby visually creating a sanctuary that counteracts the general expansiveness of the yurt. The cloth can be opaque, which creates genuine visual privacy, or it can be a gauzy fabric, to keep the room feeling open visually while still creating a sense of a personal intimacy.

I once lived in a yurt where I had a steady stream of overnight visitors. I hung shimmering translucent fabric with fishing line from the rafters above the foot of my bed. I was amazed both by

This Kirghiz-style rental yurt in Cornwall, England, incorporates elements of Central Asian design, like Persian rugs and colorful wall hangings, with furnishings made out of natural materials. A woodstove has been installed for heat, and candle lanterns are used for lighting. The colorful inner liner of orange and yellow brings warmth to the traditionally windowless interior.

how much privacy it gave without breaking up the open feeling of the yurt and how effective it was in communicating to visitors that my private space was off limits. When I wanted to open up the whole yurt to friends for candlelight evenings of music and dance, I simply pulled back the fabric and my bed became a seating area.

If burrows and nests are what you're most comfortable with, you might use partial barriers like tall shelving units, clothes racks, or a wardrobe to create lots of smaller private spaces. You might also build a cozy sleeping loft to nestle into.

If you're most comfortable with the feel of walls

A sense of different rooms within a single open yurt space can be created through the use of furnishings, screens, or hanging fabric to create privacy. The yurt pictured on this page uses lodgepole pine rafters and is made by the Canadian company Yurtco.

and a room around you, or you're living as a family in a single yurt, then you might choose to build a master bedroom and bathroom into your yurt. A loft above the bedroom can provide an extra sleeping or storage space. If you design your kitchen area to share a wall with the bathroom, the plumbing for both bathroom and kitchen can be brought up inside the shared wall.

In the fabric yurt, interior walls and rooms should be built after the yurt is erected and they should be freestanding. Walls connected to the outer trellis wall weaken the overall structural integrity of the yurt. Most yurt companies have floor plans that show a variety of wall and room configurations. A carpenter should be able to build the interior walls or rooms without difficulty since the framing process is no different from room construction in a conventional house.

In this fabric yurt, the kitchen is located against an extended wall with bedroom and bathroom on the other side and an additional loft room above.

The kitchen shares a wall (and plumbing egress) with the bathroom.

30' Yurt

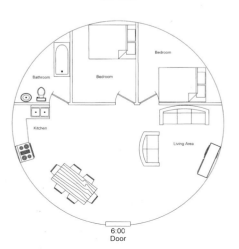

6:00
Door

Rather than building walls inside the central yurt space, this Nautilus-style frame panel yurt uses wings extending off the core yurt to contain a small kitchenette and separate bathroom.

SATELLITE YURTS AND OUTBUILDINGS

Rather than divide up a larger yurt into smaller spaces, many yurt owners choose to connect more than one yurt or to use a "satellite" system of yurts, where each yurt functions as a different room. A couple, for example, might choose to use one yurt as a living and bedroom yurt and add a second as a studio or office yurt. When children come along, another small yurt can be added as a kids' playroom.

A connecting or satellite yurt system is often combined with outbuildings for toilet and shower facilities. In cold climates, sometimes both kitchen and bathroom are placed in a single outbuilding that can be super insulated and kept warm with a thermostat-controlled propane heater. Plumbing for both kitchen and bathroom can be brought up through a shared central wall, providing additional insulation. Placing all the cold-sensitive plumbing in an outbuilding allows the larger yurt structures to remain unheated when not inhabited.

For over two decades, the members of a yurt village in Kelly, Wyoming, shared a central building with bathhouse, toilet, laundry facilities, and a large kitchen and dining area. Because the plumbing and electrical were centralized in the shared building, the live-in yurts could manage without those features, making more space available for living and office functions.

Sometimes smaller yurts are used as outbuildings, as in this Cornwall, England, bathhouse. The use of color—the matching roof liner and tub and contrasting wall liner and floor—makes this yurt especially inviting.

This Colorado family chose to cluster their yurts, providing privacy where needed and different spaces for different functions. They also created a simple outdoor room around the barbeque for family evenings together.

A family in northern California built a large tapered wall yurt as a central kitchen and family room. As the family grew, they built smaller yurt outbuildings as bedrooms for the parents and children. This arrangement provided space for both private times and family gatherings and gave the children a sense of ownership of their own satellite room. The only disadvantage was having to provide heat and power for a number of separate buildings.

Since space is often at a premium in a yurt, you may want to include outdoor spaces in your overall design. Decks and grassy areas can become hospitality spaces; a place under a tree can be set aside for meditation. You may want to design a rounded deck to continue the circular lines of the yurt.

Outdoor rooms can be created as well. Outdoor showers are common in warmer climates. I like to have more space for cooking than my yurt will allow, and I also enjoy the feeling of being outside while I cook, so from spring through fall I use an outdoor kitchen for cooking, canning, and drying herbs.

YURT INTERIORS AND FURNISHINGS

Interior design in yurts seems to be largely a matter of taste and culture. The Mongolians keep their yurts simple. The wooden framework and door are painted in bright colors with intricate designs, and chests are painted to match. Otherwise there is a monochromatic, muted color scheme and minimal decoration.

In contrast, Kirghiz yurts contain an explosion of color and pattern that includes intricately woven bands encircling the yurt inside and outside, patterned reed screens, brightly colored tassels hanging from the central ring, and colorful rugs covering the floor.

The Asian nomads place their furnishings against the wall, leaving the yurt's middle space open except for the central fire in colder seasons.

Not wanting to break up the indoor space of her Alaska yurt with walls, Elizabeth Wasserman decided to build an attached outbuilding to house the bathroom. "I wasn't clued in on square footage," she says, "and we ended up with a cabin instead of just a bathhouse." Elizabeth calls her combination yurt and cabin "the Yurbin."

Furniture, like tables and stools, are brought out as needed and then returned to the perimeter.

Likewise, in modern fabric yurts, many people keep the central space open and place furniture around the perimeter. Folding chairs and tables, or a rolling kitchen counter that can be used as needed and then put away to create more space, are commonly used.

Morgan Reiter of Oregon Yurtworks, on the other hand, recommends to his frame panel yurt clients that they situate their furniture in the middle of their yurts, thereby accentuating the feeling of being inside and looking out.

Both Japanese and Swedish designs have elements that transfer well to yurts and furnishings that are easily adapted to the needs of most yurt dwellers. North American furnishings are designed for multi-room rectilinear homes where furniture is often oversized, stationary, and intended for a single use. Japanese and Swedish furnishings, on the other hand, are lightweight, moveable, and multifunctional. The Japanese futon, for example, is lightweight and movable and serves as both sofa and bed. Swedish-designed beds may have built-in or rolling drawers beneath them, coffee tables might double as storage chests, and dining tables may fold and unfold to various shapes and sizes and include a drawer for utensils. Open storage concepts that combine function and decoration are common (for example, storing items in beautiful woven baskets instead of behind closet doors). Furnishings also come in light or muted colors that promote a feeling of openness.

The Japanese emphasis on natural materials, simplicity, and "unostentatious refinement" transfers well to yurts. Organic elements like cotton, hemp, wood, bamboo, and rice paper seem right at home

At a Scandinavian furnishings store, artist Debra Amerson found furniture that was rounded and lightweight and that could be pieced together in sections to match the circular walls of her Myurt studio.

in a yurt context, as do furnishings like screens, rice paper lanterns, and grass mats.

The Japanese design technique of using a raised floor and curtain to define private space also provides interesting possibilities for yurts, particularly when combined with the Japanese design idea of creating below-floor storage space (where stored linens or bedding, for example, provide extra floor insulation while being stored out of sight).

THE LIMITLESS POTENTIAL OF YURTS

The flexible open space of a yurt is an interior design canvas waiting for the creative expression of each yurt inhabitant. What remains constant is the welcoming embrace of the space, the interaction between inner and outer worlds, and the roof structure that lifts our vision skyward. The yurt also has an inherent ability to bring people together into a circle, which naturally engenders connection and cooperation. Perhaps the best guideline of all for living in the round is to simply amplify and enhance the natural properties of the structure, allowing the yurt itself to be the guide.

APPENDIX 1: BUILDING CODE EXCERPTS

YURTS AND BUILDING

Some states use the Uniform Building Code (UBC), but many states, provinces, and countries use the ICC (International Code Council) code books, which consist of the commercial International Building Code (IBC) and the International Residential Code (IRC). There are also subcodes, such as the International Energy Conservation Code, which add to and modify the general code books.

The excerpted sections in this appendix are drawn from the 2003 IBC (commercial code). Section 104 on the duties of building officials is the same in the commercial and residential codes; Section 3102 on membrane structures exists only in the commercial code; it defines the category for the residential code as well. The building code terminology for the fabric yurt is "membrane-covered frame structure."

As was stated earlier (pages 96–97), in order to be permitted, a yurt may have to meet requirements in the areas of snow load, seismic rating, wind speed, and fire safety, but these are dependent on location. This information comes from the local code official. Other requirements like egress and occupancy are dependent on the use of the yurt (e.g., residential or commercial).

2003 INTERNATIONAL BUILDING CODE
SECTION 104: DUTIES AND POWERS OF BUILDING OFFICIAL

104.1 GENERAL. The building official is hereby authorized and directed to enforce the provisions of this code. The building official shall have the authority to render interpretations of this code and to adopt policies and procedures in order to clarify the application of its provisions. Such interpretations, policies, and procedures shall be in compliance with the intent and purpose of this code. Such policies and procedures shall not have the effect of waiving requirements specifically provided for in this code.

104.10 MODIFICATIONS. Wherever there are practical difficulties involved in carrying out the provisions of this code, the building official shall have the authority to grant modifications for individual cases, upon application of the owner or owner's representative, provided the building official shall first find that special individual reason that makes the strict letter of this code impractical and the modification is in compliance with the intent and purpose of this code and that such modification does not lessen health, accessibility, life and fire safety, or structural requirements. The details of action granting modifications shall be recorded and entered in the files of the department of building safety.

104.11 ALTERNATIVE MATERIALS, DESIGN, AND METHODS OF CONSTRUCTION AND EQUIPMENT. The provisions of this code are not intended to prevent the installation of any material or to prohibit any design or method of construction not specifically prescribed by this code, provided that any such alternative has been approved. An alternative material, design, or method of construction shall be approved where the building official finds that the proposed design is satisfactory and complies with the intent of the provisions of this code, and that the material, method, or work offered is, for the purpose intended, at least the equivalent of that prescribed in this code in quality, strength, effectiveness, fire resistance, durability, and safety.

SECTION 3102: MEMBRANE STRUCTURES

3102.1 GENERAL. The provisions of this section shall apply to air-supported, air-inflated, membrane-covered cable and membrane-covered frame structures, collectively known as membrane structures, erected for a period of 180 days or longer. Those erected for a shorter period of time shall comply with the *International Fire Code.*

3102.2 DEFINITIONS. The following words and terms shall, for the purpose of this section and as used elsewhere in this code, have the meanings shown herein:

MEMBRANE-COVERED FRAME STRUCTURE. A non-pressurized building wherein the structure is composed of a rigid framework to support a tensioned membrane, which provides the weather barrier.

3102.7 ENGINEERING DESIGN. The structure shall be designed and constructed to sustain dead loads; loads due to tension or inflation; live loads including wind, snow, or flood and seismic loads.

2003 INTERNATIONAL ENERGY CONSERVATION CODE

101.3 INTENT. The provisions of this code shall regulate the design of building envelopes for adequate thermal resistance and low air leakage. . . . It is intended that these provisions provide flexibility to permit the use of innovative approaches and techniques to achieve effective utilization of energy.

103.1 GENERAL. The provisions of this code are not intended to prevent the use of any material, method of construction, design or insulating system not specifically prescribed herein, provided that such construction, design, or insulating system has been approved by the code official as meeting the intent of the code.

APPENDIX 2: PLATFORM CONSTRUCTION

The information in this appendix gives an idea of what is involved in platform construction for fabric yurts and the skills and materials required. However, it is very important that readers ultimately work with the plans supplied by their own yurt company.

The modern fabric yurt is designed to be placed on top of a round wooden platform, with the fabric yurt cover extending below the inside floor level of that platform in order to create a weatherproof fit. Each company has its own unique designs for both the outer wall covering and the yurt platform, and the platform must be built to conform to that design. If you are purchasing a replacement cover from a new company, be aware that platform modifications may be required.

TYPICAL YURT PLATFORM

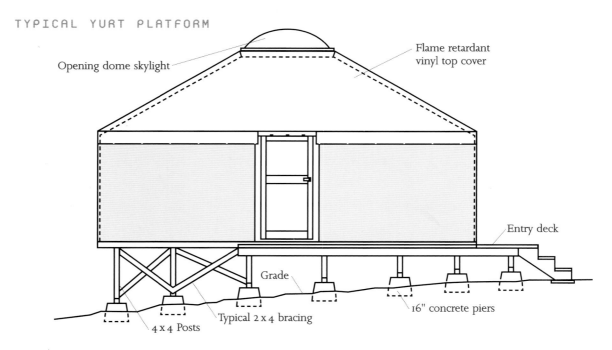

Opening dome skylight

Flame retardant vinyl top cover

Entry deck

Grade

16" concrete piers

Typical 2 x 4 bracing

4 x 4 Posts

If you plan to add an entry or surrounding deck to your platform, be sure it is placed at a lower level than the yurt platform so that the side cover can be properly attached. Platform and footings should be designed according to the conditions of the individual site and local building requirements.

MATERIALS LIST

MATERIAL	K.D. SELECT DECK	PLYWOOD SHEETS (*ALTERNATE)	CONCRETE	STANDARD & BTR FIR	EXTERIOR PLYWOOD SIDING	STANDARD & BTR FIR
DIMENSION	2 x 6	4' x 8'	16"	4 x 6	3/8" x 6"	2 x 6
DESCRIPTION	T&G DECKING	1 1/8" T&G PLYWOOD DECKING	PIERS	BEAMS	DRIP EDGE	PERIM. BLOCKING
DIA. UNIT	(LIN. FT.)	(SHEETS)	N/A	(LIN. FT.)	(LIN. FT.)	(LIN. FT.)
12'	300	6	11	36	38	20
14'	400	8	13	53	44	30
16'	520	8	13	57	51	36
20'	840	12	16	88	63	46
24'	1225	18	20	112	76	74
30'	1800	24	30	179	95	96

This list of materials is specific to Pacific Yurts–style platforms and is approximate; actual usage varies according to cutting efficiency and design changes. For flooring, 4' x 8' x 1 1/8" tongue-and-groove (T&G) plywood may be substituted for the 2 x 6 tongue-and-groove select decking materials specified above.

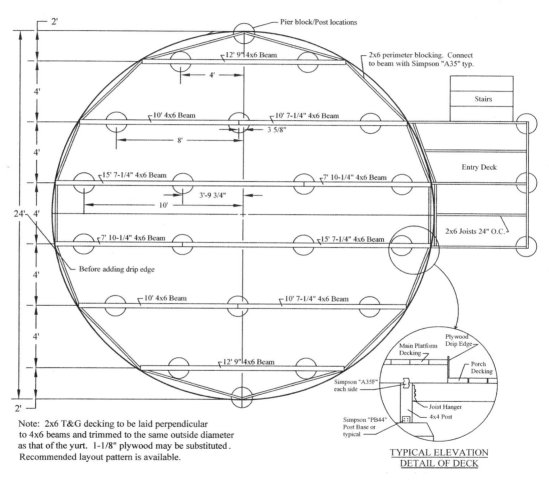

Note: 2x6 T&G decking to be laid perpendicular
to 4x6 beams and trimmed to the same outside diameter
as that of the yurt. 1-1/8" plywood may be substituted.
Recommended layout pattern is available.

TYPICAL ELEVATION
DETAIL OF DECK

This plan comes with detailed written instructions, which you should have in hand before building. Unless you are skilled, it's a good idea to enlist the help of an experienced carpenter.

Note that footing design and placement and platform construction should reflect the conditions of the individual site.

APPENDIX 3:
WOODSTOVE AND CHIMNEY INSTALLATION

There are many ways to install a woodstove and chimney. This diagram from Pacific Yurts shows one method. Additional diagrams are available on other company Web sites.

The specifications given in this diagram are intended only as a guideline. For more information please contact your stove dealer or local fire marshal.

SAFETY RECOMMENDATIONS

o— Purchase the correct size stove for your yurt. Remember that round rooms are more efficient to heat than square, especially when there are no dividing walls.

o— Place your stove on the leeward (downwind) side of the yurt to minimize wind coming down the pipe and to blow sparks and ashes coming out of the chimney away from the yurt rather than towards it.

o— Keep the stove at a safe distance from combustible surfaces. Follow the manufacturer's recommendations for clearance distances.

o— Use the right stovepipe. Most yurt company flashing is designed to be used with a six-inch (inside diameter) insulated pipe (Metalbestos or equivalent), rated to be two inches from a combustible surface.

o— Invest in a small fire extinguisher.

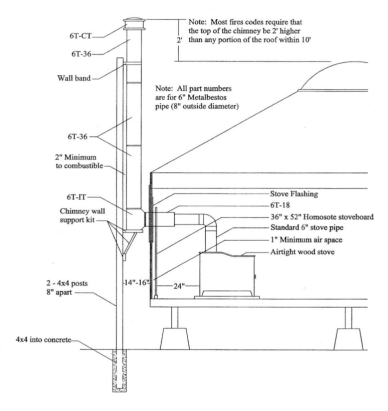

Note: Most fires codes require that the top of the chimney be 2' higher than any portion of the roof within 10'

Note: All part numbers are for 6" Metalbestos pipe (8" outside diameter)

6T-CT
6T-36
Wall band
6T-36
2" Minimum to combustible
6T-IT
Chimney wall support kit
2 - 4x4 posts 8" apart
14"-16"
24"
4x4 into concrete

Stove Flashing
6T-18
36" x 52" Homosote stoveboard
Standard 6" stove pipe
1" Minimum air space
Airtight wood stove

o— Clean the stovepipe at regular (e.g., monthly) intervals.

o— Seek advice from your woodstove dealer or call your yurt company.

RESOURCE GUIDE

The Resources Guide contains four sections:

- o— Yurt Companies and Financing
- o— Yurt Plans
- o— General Yurt Resources
- o— Homesteading and Sustainable Living

Each section of this guide contains both standard and online resources. Because contact information changes, multiple access points have been supplied where possible.

Updated resource information and links will be posted on the author's Web site, www.yurtinfo.org.

YURT COMPANIES

A word about phone numbers: the country code is listed in parentheses, except for North American companies. To call within most countries you will need to drop the country code and add a zero before the number. The country code for the United States and Canada is "1."

Modern Fabric Yurts

Colorado Yurt Company
PO Box 1626
28 W. South 4th St.
Montrose, CO 81401
Tel. 1-800-288-3190 • 970-240-2111
www.coloradoyurt.com
> Manufacturing yurts and tipis since the 1970s. Advance Jurten (www.jurten.de) is the company's German subsidiary.

GoYurt Shelters
Tel. 1-877-4GOYURT • 818-625-6156
www.goyurt.com • info@goyurt.com
> Truly portable yurt that can be set up by two people in thirty minutes.

Nomad Shelter
389 Grubstake Ave., #1
Homer, AK 99603
Tel. 907-235-0132
www.nomadshelter.com • nomadger@alaska.net
> Alaskan yurts with Lexan panel skylight for a central stove.

Outback Yurts
PO Box 18
Stanley, ID 83278
Tel. 208-774-3324
getaway@sawtoothguides.com
> Custom backcountry yurts designed for heavy snow loads.

Pacific Yurts
77456 Hwy. 99 S.
Cottage Grove, OR 97424
Tel. 800-944-0240 • 541-942-9435
www.yurts.com • info@yurts.com
> Largest manufacturer of modern fabric yurts worldwide.

Rainier Yurts
18435 Olympic Ave. S.
Seattle, WA 98188
Tel. 866-839-8787 • 425-981-1253
www.rainieryurts.com • sales@rainieryurts.com
> Yurt options include interchangeable wall panels and framed windows.

Red Mountain Lodge Works
Lake City, CO
Tel. 970-944-2639
grayj@lakecity.net
  Solar yurts with a south-facing clear front.

Shelter Design, LLC
477 Seventeen Mile Rd.
Troy, MT 59935
Tel. 406-295-5691
shelterdesign@yahoo.com

Tuckamore Yurts
33 West St.
Corner Brook, NL Canada 82H 2y6
Tel. 709-639-5678
www.tuckamoreyurts.ca • diamondelle@nf.aibn.com
  Yurts designed for the harsh Newfoundland climate.

Yourte Contemporaine
18, Rue Sebastien LeTourneux,
44450 Saint-Julien de concelles
LeTourneux, France
www.yourte-contemporaine.fr • t.rouelle@yourte-contemporaine.fr
  Rainier Yurts' French subsidiary.

Yurtco Manufacturing
Canadian Yurts
5784 Byrne Rd.
Burnaby, BC, Canada, V5J 3J4
Tel. 866-4YURTCO • 604-629-2982
www.yurtco.com • info@yurtco.com
  Canada's leading manufacturer of yurts, with log rafters.
  Long-term commercial rentals available from sister
  company Canadian Yurts.

Traditional Yurts

Albion Canvas Co.
Unit 6, Barkingdon Business Park
Staverton, Totnes
Devon, UK TQ9 6AN
Tel. 0845-456-9290 (local rate) • (44) 1803-762230
www.albioncanvas.co.uk
  Kirghiz-style yurts, groundsheets, and custom covers
  for self-built yurt frames.

Atelier des Trois Yourtes
Charles Leys
6 rue des vergers
35 330 LES BRÚLAIS (Bretagne)
Tel. (33) 299-078478 • (33) 299-924782
www.yourtes.fr • charles@yourtes.fr
  Kirghiz-style yurts, imported furnishings, and accessories.

Bruton Yurt Company
Jonathan and Caroline Morriss
The Barn
Higher Backway
Bruton
Somerset, UK BA10 0DW
Tel. (44) 1963-31955 (workshop) • (44) 7710-210289 (mobile)
www.brutonyurts.com • byc@btinternet.com
  Yurt building and rental.

FAM Tents Deutschland
www.friereit.de

FAM ZELTWELT GmbH
Tomas and Bernadette Beco
Grossholz/Postfach 158
8253 Diessenhofen TG
Schweiz
Tel. (41) 52-657-5858 • (41) 79-620-6506 (cell)
www.zeltwelt.ch

Handmade Hardwood Yurts
Steve Place and Francine Isaacs
Bont Glan Tanat
Llanrhaeadr Ym Mochnant
nr Oswestry, Wales SY100AF
Tel. (44) 1691-780639
www.yurts.fsnet.co.uk • steveplace@yurts.fsnet.co.uk
 Turkic-style yurts and Alachi; also groundsheets and felt
 insulation.

Liber Tente
Avenue Saint Roch
13 930 Aureille
France
Tel. (33) 6-23-14-40-65 • (33) 6-24-97-88-83
www.vivrelayourte.fr • vivrelayourte@free.fr

Mongolian Artisans' Aid Foundation (MAAF)
Mr. Cristo Gomez
Ulaanbaatar 28
PO Box 329
Mongolia
Tel. 976-11-311051 • 206-888-4286 (for U.S.
callers)
www.samarmagictours.com
 Imports gers made by Mongolian artisans, traditional
 furnishings, and stoves.

The Mongolian Yurt
www.mongolyurt.com
 Imports Mongolian yurts to the United States and Germany.

Turkoman Gers
Hal Wynne-Jones
Twizzlestone Piece, Off Limekiln Lane
Bisley
Gloucestershire, GL6 7NW UK
Tel. (44) 1452-771212
www.turkoman-gers.co.uk
 Rental gers for special occasions and Turkic-style gers
 for sale.

Woodland Yurts Co.
Paul King
80 Coleridge Vale Rd. South
Clevedon
North Somerset, UK BS21 6PG
Tel. 44 (0) 1275-879705
www.woodlandyurts.freeserve.co.uk •
yurts@woodlandyurts.co.uk
 Mongolian and Turkic yurts since 1991. Plans available
 on Web site.

Workshop Under the Hill
Alexandr Sprado
Povltavská 41
250 67 Klecany, Czech Republic
Tel. (420) 723-257-915
www.yourtent.com • workshop@yourtent.com
 Traditional yurts. Web site in Czech, German, and
 English with forums and an extensive photo gallery.

World Tents
David Field
Redfield
Buckingham Rd.
Winslow, Bucks, UK MK18 3LZ
Tel. 44 (0) 1296-714555
www.worldtents.co.uk • info@worldtents.co.uk
 Variety of tents, including yurts.

The Yurt Workshop
Robert Matthews
C/Naranjillos 16
Narila, Granada, 18448 Spain
Tel. (34) 958-76-81-21
www.yurtworkshop.com
 Mongolian and Turkic yurts. Extensive Web site.

Yurtworks
Tim Hutton
Greyhayes
St Breward
Bodmin
Cornwall, UK PL30 4LP
Tel. (44) 1208-850670
www.yurtworks.co.uk • info@yurtworks.co.uk
  Kirghiz-style yurts, rentals, and Cornish yurt holidays.

Tapered Wall Yurts

JADE Craftsman Builders
Dan Neumeyer
Tel. 360-331-2964
www.jadedesignbuild.com • dneumeyer@aol.com
  Dan integrates yurts based on Bill Coperthwaite's designs
  into standard building designs.

The Yurt Foundation
Bill Coperthwaite
Dickinson's Reach
Machiasport, ME 04655
www.yurtinfo.org/yurtfoundation.php
  Established in 1971, the Yurt Foundation works with
  groups to build yurts as a part of a community or edu-
  cational experience. The foundation also sells yurt plans.

Frame Panel Yurts

California Yurts
David Raitt
Talmage, CA
Tel. 1-888-CAL-YURT
www.yurtpeople.com
  Original designer of modern engineered frame panel yurt.

Douglas Fir Yurts
32470 Mill Canyon Rd.
Davenport, WA 91122
Tel. 509-725-0307
goldberryherbs@yahoo.com
  Custom frame panel yurts up to twenty-four feet;
  emphasis on recycled materials.

Goulburn Yurtworks
12 Copford Rd.
Bradfordville, Goulburn
PO Box 645
Goulburn NSW 2580 Australia
Tel. (61) 2-4821-5931
www.yurtworks.com.au
  Frame panel yurts sold as kits or erected for the client.

Mandala Custom Homes
Box 234
Nelson, BC, Canada VIL 5P9
Tel. 866-352-5503 • 250-352-5582
www.mandalahomes.com • info@mandala-
homes.com
  Canada's round home builder, emphasizing respon-
  sibly harvested wood and nontoxic materials.

Oregon Yurtworks
1285 Wallis St.
Eugene, OR 97402
Tel. 800-211-8470 • 541-343-5330
www.yurtworks.com
  Prefabricated frame panel yurts sold as kits or erected
  for client.

Smiling Woods Yurts
Twisp, WA
Tel. 509-997-2180
www.smilingwoodsyurts.com • michael@smiling
woodsyurts.com
  Frame panel yurt kits with a metal roof. Kits are available separately and can be added to cob or strawbale
  buildings.

Related Designs

Bamboo Living Homes
120 Hana Hwy., #9, Ste. 133
Paia, HI 96799
Tel. 808-572-1007
www.bambooliving.com • bamboo@bamboo
technologies.com
  Prefabricated, panelized octagon homes of bamboo.

Geo-Lite Systems
6118 W. 77th St.
Los Angeles, CA 90045
Tel. 310-216-0410
www.geolitesystems.com • info@geolitesystems.com
  Prefabricated yurt-type structures with a steel frame,
  wooden wall panels, and a fabric roof.

Red Sky Shelters
2002 Riverside Dr., Loft H
Asheville, NC 28804
Tel. 828-258-8417
www.redskyshelters.com • isis@redskyshelters.com
  The Yome combines the shape of the yurt with the
  principles of the geodesic dome.

Yurt Financing

Commercial enterprises (like campgrounds and
resorts) may be able to finance yurts through business or equipment loan companies. The two companies listed on the next page have experience in
financing yurts for commercial purposes.

Clear View Financial
64 Basin St. SW
Ephrata, WA 98823
Tel. 888-408-8805
www.clearviewfinancial.com
mike@clearviewfinancial.com
  Specializes in the camping industry.

Pinnacle Business Financing
Joe Bertram
159 S. Worthen, Ste. 300
Wenatchee, WA. 98801
Tel. 888-223-2600
www.pinnaclecap.com • jbertram@pinnaclecap.com

YURT PLANS

Each book or set of plans has its own angle. The
Coxes' plans, which use modern materials, are
designed for year-round habitation. UK designers
work with modified Turkic or Mongolian designs.
Society of Creative Anachronism (SCA) members
are primarily interested in historical replication and
build Mongolian-style yurts for camping at reenactment events. Bill Coperthwaite's tapered wall yurts
are the only wooden yurt plans available, although
Geo-Lite Systems has plans for a hybrid yurt-type
structure that uses wooden wall panels.

BOOKS

In The Real Mongol Ger Book, Dutch yurt-maker Froit
shares professional secrets learned from Mongolian
ger makers, with a few concessions for differences
in climate and Western needs. The handcrafted and
self-published book can be ordered online at
www.nooitmeerhaast.nl/tsteng/the-book.html.
Froit may be contacted at info@nooitmeerhaast.nl.

Paul King's book The Complete Yurt Handbook (Bath:
Eco-Logic Books, 2001) includes plans for traditional
yurts. It can be ordered online at www.wood-
landyurts.co.uk.

The fact sheet How to Build a Yurt by Steve Place, with
instructions for a Turkic-style yurt, is available
through the Centre for Alternative Technology at
www.cat.org.uk.

For instructions on felting, see Felt: New Directions for
an Ancient Craft by Gunilla Paetau Sjoberg. Translated
by Patricia Spark (Loveland, CO: Interweave Press,
1996).

In Build a Yurt (New York: Sterling Publishing Co,
1974, currently out of print), Len Charney explains
how he built an early version of Bill Coperthwaite's
tapered wall yurt.

The Portable Yurt, the original modern fabric yurt plans, can be ordered for $25 (post paid) from Chuck and Laurel Cox:

Tuckaway Farm
59 Randall Rd.
Lee, NH 03824

Three sets of tapered wall yurt plans are available from Bill Coperthwaite. Send a check or money order and a note stating which plans you want to:

The Yurt Foundation
Dickinson's Reach
Machiasport, ME 04655

Plan costs are as follows:

o— $25 for "The Little Yurt." Plans come in three dimensions: Tiny (10' diameter), Little (12' diameter), and Standard (17' diameter).

o— $50 for "The Concentric Yurt" (1,000 square feet, 36' diameter).

o— $75 for "The Family Yurt" (2,700 square feet, 54' diameter).

Geo-Lite Systems sells a set of plans for their twelve-, fourteen-, and sixteen-panel yurt-style structures, which use metal framing, wooden wall panels, and a fabric roof. Plans can be ordered at www.geolitesystems.com/plans.html.

online downloads

Paul King shares a set of plans for a Mongolian ger online. To download, go to www.woodlandyurts.co.uk/Yurt_Facts/ Downloads.html.

The Mongolian Yurt, Part I and Part II may be downloaded from the SCA Publication Sacred Spaces, Issue #9, at www.currentmiddleages.org/ tents/toc.htm.

The Construction of a Yurt, an online paper written by an SCA member with details on yurt specs and components, can be downloaded at www.pbm.com/~lindahl/articles/yurt.

How We Made Our Own Gher: How to Avoid Our Mistakes, notes from an SCA project, can be downloaded at www.cco.net/~str8jkt/yurt.html.

Yurt Notes, a set of building notes with instructions for calculating the mathematics of yurt components (and a calculator to do the work for you) can be found at http://housing.byrene.com/yurt_notes.

Instructions for creating yurt felts can be found in the FAQ section at www.peak.org/~spark/feltlistFAQ.html.

materials

For a listing of UK and European suppliers that includes fabric manfacturers and sewing and welding supplies, see www.tents-for-sale.co.uk.

workshops

If you want to build a tapered wall yurt, Bill Coperthwaite will lead a workshop in which eight to twelve people construct a simple yurt in six days. To contact Bill with details of your project or to find out about upcoming workshops, write to:

The Yurt Foundation
Dickinson's Reach
Machiasport, ME 04655

Graham McLaren of Douglas Fir Yurts in Washington State leads building workshops for frame panel yurts. To contact Graham, call 509-725-0307, or write:

Douglas Fir Yurts
32470 Mill Canyon Rd.
Davenport, WA 91122

Circle Houses: Yurts, Tipis and Benders. Pearson, David. The House That Jack Built Series. White River Junction, Vermont: Chelsea Green Publishing, 2001. (*Yurts, Tipis and Benders,* London: Gaia Books Ltd., 2001.)

> Lots of yurt stories, mainly from the UK, with instructions for building a Mongolian-style yurt.

The Changing World of Mongolia's Nomads. Goldstein, Melvyn, and Cynthia Beall. Berkeley: University of California Press, 1994.

> Anthropologists document a herding cooperative. Book features beautiful photographs.

The Complete Yurt Handbook. King, Paul. Batn: Eco-Logic Books 2001.

> Includes instructions on how to make both Mongolian and Turkic yurts. Emphasis is on traditional Central Asian yurts.

Felt Tents and Pavilions: The Nomadic Tradition and Its Interaction with Princely Tentage. Andrews, Peter Alford. 2 vols. London: Melisende, 1999.

> Vol. I covers the nomadic Mongolian tradition, and Vol. II covers "princely tentage" on the Indian subcontinent in the medieval period. Includes over 275 photos, illustrations, and color plates.

Home Work: Handbuilt Shelter. Kahn, Lloyd. Bolinas, CA: Shelter Publications, 2004.

> A nice section on Bill Coperthwaite's yurts and some information on Mongolian gers.

Mongolian Cloud Houses: How to Make a Yurt and Live Comfortably. Kuehn, Dan Frank. Bolinas, CA: Shelter Publications, 2006.

> Drawings and step-by-step instructions for building a low-cost fabric yurt with a bamboo framework.

"Nature's Education." *Fabric Architecture Magazine.* May and June 2000.

> An article about yurts designed for a park in Japan, with an unusual structural design and a Teflon-coated fabric covering.

Nomad Tent Types of the Middle East: Part 1, Framed Tents. Andrews, Peter Alford. 3 vols. Wiesbaden, Germany: L. Ludwig Reichert Verlag, 1997.

> Scholarly work on the Central Asian Turkic yurts by the world's leading authority. Vol. 1 contains written material, Vol. 2 has the accompanying photographs and diagrams, and Vol. 3 contains maps.

Nomads of Eurasia. Basilov, Vladimir N., ed. Translated by Mary Fleming Zirin. Seattle and London: Natural History Museum of Los Angeles County in association with the University of Washington Press, 1989.

> History of the Central Asian nomads with a section on yurts and lots of historical photographs of people and crafts.

The Real Mongol Ger Book. Froit. Available through www.nooitmeerhaast.nl/txteng/the-book.html.

> Construction details and background information for an authentic Mongolian ger. Handmade book that includes samples of wood, felt, and canvas.

Shelter. Easton, Bob. Edited by Lloyd Kahn. Bolinas, CA: Shelter Publications, 1973. Reprint Random House, 1990.

Shelter II. Kahn, Lloyd. Bolinas, CA: Shelter Publications, 1978.

> Shelter I and II are classic works on shelter worldwide, with chapters on yurts in each.

Tents: Architecture of the Nomads. Faegre, Torvald. London: Anchor Books, 1979. (Currently out of print.)

> Beautifully written and often profound. Hand-drawn illustrations by Faegre throughout.

Tipis and Yurts: Authentic Designs for Circular Structures. Blue Evening Star. Asheville, NC: Lark Books, 1995.
> The first yurt book. Features a Southwest-style, tipi-based yurt design.

The White House of Khurasan: The Felt Tents of the Iranian Yomut and Gökle'n. Andrews, Peter Alford. Iran XI, London: Jarmal of the Paritisn Institute of Persian Studies, 1973, 93–110.
> Detailed information on yurt-building traditions of Iranian tribes.

FiLMS

Herdsmen. Executive Producer Wei Bin. A Co-production of China Central Television and Xinjiang Grandscape Telecon, 2000. Order through docued@der.org.
> A ninety-minute documentary in the Kazak language with English subtitles.

Mujaan (The Craftsman). Produced and directed by Chris McKee, Ragcha Media, 2004. Available at www.mujaan.com.
> A beautifully crafted story, 25 minutes long, of Mongolian nomads building a ger.

The Silk Road film series (6 vols). Produced by NHK Enterprises. Available through Central Park Media. www.centralparkmedia.com. Tel. 212-977-7456.
> Some segments on the Central Asian nomads with scenes of yurts. See especially "Where Horses Fly Like the Wind" in the first series.

The Story of the Weeping Camel. Byambasuren Dava and Luigi Falorni, Directors. National Geographic World Films, 2005.
> This moving tale of a Mongolian family unfolds in and around their ger.

Wild Horses of Mongolia. PBS Nature, 2003. www.pbs.org/wnet/nature/mongolia.
> Julia Roberts spends several weeks living in a ger with a nomadic Mongolian family.

online resources

GENERAL INFORMATION

Yurt Info
www.yurtinfo.org
> Author's Web site with FAQs, resource updates, a forum, and a classified section for used yurts.

Yurt Quest
www.chaingang.org/yurtquest/index.html
> The original yurt information page.

Stephan's Florilegium
www.florilegium.org, under "Structures" and then "Yurts."
> Society of Creative Anachronism (SCA) discussions gathered in one place.

Interview with Bill Coperthwaite
www.herondance.org/Bill_Coperthwaite_W9.cfm

Peter Andrews
www.peterandrews.info
> Andrews has spent forty years studying traditional yurts and nomad tents.

CONSTRUCTION

Many of the yurt company Web sites feature slide shows of deck or yurt building. See the "Yurt Companies" section on the first page of this Resource Guide.

Lars' Yurt Page
www.rdrop.com/~glacier/yurt.htm
> Photographs of deck construction and setting up a fabric yurt.

Mongol Yurt
www.mongolyurt.com/en/reports/ammertal.html
> A German couple installs a Mongolian ger in their backyard. Site includes helpful hints.

Feltmakers List FAQ
www.peak.org/~spark/feltlistFAQ.html

Information on Felt Tents, Yurts, Gers
www.peak.org/~spark/felttents,yurts,gers.html
A felters' discussion of yurts.

The Storytelling Yurt
www.scottishstorytellingyurt.co.uk

FORUMS
Yurtinfo
www.yurtinfo.org

Yourtent
www.yourtent.com
International forum in three languages.

Yurt Workshop
www.yurtworkshop.com

FURNISHINGS
IKEA Swedish design
www.ikea.com
Simple and nomad-friendly designs.

Lehmans Non-Electric Catalog
www.lehmans.com

HISTORY
Land of Genghis Khan
www.nationalgeographic.com/genghis
A writer and photographer travel in the footsteps of the great Khan.

TRAVEL
Boojum Expeditions
www.boojum.com
Travel Central Asia on horseback, stay in a yurt, and meet locals. Includes a list of resources on Mongolia.

Oregon State Parks
www.oregon.gov/OPRD/PARKS/cabins.html
Over two hundred yurts in more than twenty parks.

HOMESTEADING AND SUSTAINABLE LIVING
Books

The Composting Toilet System Book. Del Porto, David, and Carol Steinfeld. Concord, MA: CEPP, 2000.
A practical guide to composting toilet systems.

The Good Life. Nearing, Helen, and Scott Nearing. White River Junction, VT: Chelsea Green, 1989.
Classic work on homesteading by the pioneers of the "back to the land" movement.

The Humanure Handbook. Jenkins, Joseph. Grove City, PA: Jenkins Publishing, 1999.
Practical solutions for waste management.

The Natural House: A Complete Guide to Healthy, Energy-Efficient, Environmental Homes. Chiras, Daniel D. White River Junction, VT: Chelsea Green, 2000.
Chapter 15, "Site Considerations," contains an invaluable section on siting (pages 385–419). There is also helpful information on alternative energy and utilities and a comprehensive resource section.

periodicals and catalogs

Home Power Magazine
PO Box 520
Ashland, OR 97520
Tel. 800-707-6585 • 541-512-0201 (outside the US)
www.homepower.com
hp@homepower.com
The hands-on journal of homemade power.

Lehman's Non-Electric Catalog
Lehman Hardware and Appliances, Inc.
PO Box 41
Kidron, OH 44636
Tel. 888-438-5346
www.lehmans.com
   Everything you need to live with little or no electricity.

Permaculture Activist
PO Box 1209
Black Mountain, NC 28711
Tel. 828-669-6336
www.permacultureactivist.net
   North American quarterly permaculture journal.

Permaculture Magazine
www.permaculture.co.uk

www.gaia.org
   Quarterly journal of the Permaculture Association of Great Britain.

Real Goods Catalog and Institute for Solar Living
13771 S. Hwy. 101
Hopland, CA 95449
Tel. 707-744-2017

organizations

Building for Health Materials Center
Box 1113
Carbondale, CO 81623
Tel. 800-292-4838
   Natural-building supplies and nontoxic building materials.

Center for Alternative Technology
Machynlleth
Powys, SY20 9AZ, UK
Tel. (44) 1654-705950
www.cat.org.uk
   Europe's leading eco-centre with books, pamphlets, a demonstration site, and workshops on every aspect of sustainable living.

Gourmet Adobe
HC 78 Box 9811
Ranchos De Taos, NM 87557
Tel. 505-758-7251
   Adobe-expert Carole Crews teaches workshops on adobe floors, plasters, and finishes.

Solar Energy International (SEI)
PO Box 715
Carbondale, CO 81623
Tel. 970-963-8855
www.solarenergy.org • sei@solarenergy.org
   Workshops and an online newsletter on alternative energy.

web sites

Backwoods Solar Electric Systems
www.backwoodssolar.com

Chelsea Green Publishing
www.chelseagreen.com
   Books on sustainable living.

Dirt Cheap Builders Catalog
www.dirtcheapbuilder.com
   Books on homesteading and sustainable building.

Eco-logic Books
www.eco-logicbooks.com
   UK distributor of sustainable books.

New Society Publishers
www.newsociety.com
   Books on sustainable living.

Real Goods Renewable Energy Systems
www.realgoods.com
   Off-grid and sustainable product lines.

ENDNOTES

chapter 1: what's a yurt?

1 Steve Place's fact sheet *How to Build a Yurt* is available through the Centre for Alternative Technology, www.cat.org.uk.

2 In his book *Circle Houses*, David Pearson gives examples of benders and yurts being used as part of activist demonstrations. See www.jurte.ch for the story of Jurtendorf village, a nomadic yurt community in Switzerland.

3 There are lovely photographs of yurts made with the help of school children in Sweden in Gunilla Sjoberg's volume *New Directions for Felt, an Ancient Craft* (Interweave Press, 1996).

4 This expanded spacing is possible because of the greater tensile strength of the canvas that most European yurt makers are using for their covering. Rob Matthews of the Yurt Workshop in Spain suggests that the closer Central Asian spacing helps avoid compression of the felt; too wide of spacing between rafters would create a cold leak and consequent condensation. The closer Central Asian spacing of trellis and rafters also strengthens the yurt roof and increases its snow-load capacity.

chapter 2: ancient paths

1 The term *Turkic* applies to a collection of related languages used by a large tribal lineage that also shares religious and social customs. The Turkic peoples include tribal groups living in countries from Iran in the west to eastern Mongolia, south into Afghanistan, and north to the western part of Siberia. Some of the more prominent tribal groups are Turkmen, Kazakhs, and Kyrgyz, but many other tribes are included as well. These tribes live in the countries that bear their names, but their reach extends beyond national borders. Like their neighbors the Mongols, their tribal life as nomadic pastoralists has enabled them to succeed in the vast near-desert mountain steppes of Central Asia, a land considered uninhabitable by most.

2 According to V. Basilov, "a dwelling with the outline of a yurt is depicted in a painting in a Crimean crypt that dates from the third century BC." Basilov, *Nomads of Eurasia* (Seattle: University of Washington Press, 1989), 98–99.

3 In the fifth century BC, the use of felt by nomads was so widespread that the Chinese referred to the Central Asian steppes as "the land of felt." See Basilov, 34–35, and Gunilla Sjoberg, *New Directions for Felt, an Ancient Craft* (Loveland, CO: Interweave Press, 1996), 6–7, 23. Some of the earliest archaeological findings come from burial sites (called *kurgan*) that were frozen by permafrost over two thousand years ago in the Altai highlands of Siberia. When archeologists thawed the burial mounds, which date from 600–200 BC, they found high art expressed in fabric, felt, wood, and gold. Felt objects included wall hangings, articles of clothing, and decorated saddle blankets. See Basilov, 34–35. Many of the felting techniques used by the Altai people twenty-five hundred years ago appear to be the same techniques used by nomads today.

4 "Little goes to waste in traditional nomadic life. There is respect both for the material and for the effort invested in working it. Felts are passed down to poorer relatives or dependents, and perhaps cut down for use on smaller tent types, before ending their existence in camel pack saddles, or being re-felted for backing woven rugs. Struts and roof wheels, even trellises, may be downgraded for use in rib tents or vaulted tents, or old trellises can be used as hurdles for fencing a fold." Peter Alford Andrews, *Nomad Tent Types in the Middle East: Part I, Framed Tents.* (Wiesbaden, Germany: L. Reichert Verlag, 1997), 13.

5 Muhammad ibn Khavand Shah, called Mirkhwand, quoted in Peter Alford Andrews, *Felt Tents and Pavilions: The Nomadic Tradition and Its Interaction with Princely Tentage*, vol. I (London: Melisende, 1999), 546. (Hereafter, this volume is referred to as FT&P.) The Durrani Pashtun people claim that their black tent was conceived by Abraham, while the yurt of the neighboring Aymaq tribes was devised by Sheytan (Satan). See Andrews, *Nomad Tent Types*, 11.

6 Po Chu-I (AD 778–846), English version by Peter Alford Andrews, FT&P, 152. See also Basilov, 57.

7 Ahmad ibn Abu Ya'qub, *Kitab al-Buldan*. Date of writing unknown; his work was first edited in AD 891. Quoted in Andrews, FT&P, 180.

8 According to Peter Alford Andrews, *The Secret History* (oldest extant Mongolian history) was "probably composed in 1228, with later additions. The date is still discussed, but de Rachewiltz is one of the leading experts with this conclusion." Quoted from notes provided by Andrews to the author.

9 Temujin's success was due in part to nomadic social structure. "We are dealing with nomadic societies....They were not states in the sense that we are used to in sedentary societies. They were confederations...made up of a changing composition of clans....They were not...linguistically identical, but they were culturally identical insofar as they were nomads and had an economic, social, and military organization that was compatible with that of their conquerors." James Bosson, "Who are the Mongols and Why?" in T. Bartholomew, *Mongolia: The Legacy of Chingiz Khan* (San Francisco: Thames and Hudson, 1995), 8.

10 "The logic of this procedure is clearer when it is understood that the army as a mass was limited by the speed of the carts carrying its tents and baggage: it was not really in a position to pursue and harass the inhabitants as the advance guard could." Andrews, FT&P, 1296.

11 Because families were together during the long winter encampment, the army was able to continually advance without ever having to return to a central base for supplies or to visit family. Bosson, 8.

12 Giovanni de Piano Carpini. Quoted in Andrews, FT&P, 465.

13 Willem van Rubruck, 1253–55, described in Andrews, FT&P, 492–94.

14 Marco Polo. Described in Andrews, FT&P, 468ff, 492–94.

15 Rasid al-Din. Quoted in Andrews, FT&P, 549.

16 The great camp under Abu Sa'id (1316–35) had yurts of varying sizes standing pitched and available for hire. From Hsu T'ing's report of 1235–36. Andrews, FT&P, 548.

17 "Then as now, tents were the women's charge. It was the women who drove the carts, placed dwellings on the carts and took them down again, made the felt and covered the dwellings." Rubruck, summarized in Andrews, FT&P, 558.

18 Marco Polo. Quoted in Andrews, FT&P, 497.

19 "Genghis Khan and his descendants were buried in tombs which had left no visible trace.... Somewhere ahead of me the warrior shepherd slept beneath a forest glade which the wolf glided across at dusk and where swallows flitted in the morning shadows. The Mongols had not sought to conquer nature but to remain a part of it." Jasper Becker, The Lost Country: Mongolia Revealed (Sceptre, 1993), 211. The graves were also left unmarked to prevent pillage.

20 From September through February, Kublai Khan's court stayed at their winter palace in the Royal City. From March through May, they were in hunting camp. June through August were spent at the summer palace. As observed by Marco Polo, described in Andrews, FT&P, 1295–96.

21 These differences in style, components, and usage are detailed in Peter Alford Andrews's comprehensive study Nomad Tent Types of the Middle East: Part I, Framed Tents. 2 vols. (Wiesbaden, Germany: L. Reichert Verlag, 1997).

22 The term yurt comes from Russian usage. It was most likely adopted from the Tatar language, adapted with a feminine ending to become yurta and then applied to the nomadic dwelling of the Central Asian steppes. This is not, however, the word the Central Asian tribes use to refer to their portable homes. Basilov, 101.

See also Andrews, Nomad Tent Types, 5: "The word yurt is misleading: most Westerners use it in the belief that it is a native term for the trellis tent when it is not.... The Russian original, yurta, is a misapplication of the Turkic yurt meaning 'territory' or 'camp site,' but never 'tent.'...The real Turkic names for the tent, ev, öy, or üy, simply mean 'dwelling,' just as Mongolian ger does."

"As to the term for tent, üy (uiy) is right for Qazaq, Qirgiz, Qaraqalpaq, and Bashkir; the Türkmen term is öy and Tuvan is ög." Quoted from notes provided by Peter Alford Andrews to author.

23 "The basic distinction between white felts as the expression of purity and fertility and the dark felts for those who can do no better remains and is valid for the whole of Central Asia. It is . . . largely a question of wealth." Quoted from notes provided by Peter Alford Andrews to author.

24 Yevgheny Sorokin, The Kirghiz Pattern (Kurdistan: 1986). The book has wonderful photographs of Kirghiz craftwork and yurts.

25 The Siberian tipi, called ursa by the Buryats, has a much lower (or flatter) profile than the tipi of the North American native tribes. The Buryat log ger bears a strong resemblance to one style of the Navajo hogan.

26 "This is the case except in Manchuria and Kalmukia where rush mats are common." Quoted from notes provided by Peter Alford Andrews to author.

27 The roof wheel and door are typically made of elm or birch. The practice of using fully settled, skilled workers dates back at least to the thirteenth century when a Chinese envoy noted that Chinese specialists near Beijing were manufacturing all the Mongol collapsible tents. Peter Alford Andrews, Nomad Tent Types, 12.

28 Gunilla Sjoberg, 54. Some of the earliest archeological findings of felt come from burial sites (called kurgan) that were frozen by permafrost over two thousand years ago in the Altai highlands of Siberia. When archeologists thawed the burial mounds, which date from 600–200 BC, they found high art expressed in fabric, felt, wood, and gold. Felt objects included wall hangings, articles of clothing, and decorated saddle blankets. See Basilov, 34–35. Many of the felting techniques used by these Altai people twenty-five hundred years ago appear to be the same techniques used by nomads today.

29 According to Peter Alford Andrews, a 62 strut (or 62 head) tent requires 132 kg of wool, or as many as 190 fleeces of the second shearing. Andrews, "The White House of Khurasan," Journal of Persian Studies, 99.

30 Li Chich-Ch'ang mentions that among Genghis Kahn's precautions against offending the water spirits he had forbidden the Mongols to make fresh felt in the summer. A. Róna-Tas, "Felt-Making in Mongolia," in Acta Orientalia Hung, XVI (1963), 200, quoted in Andrews, FT&P, 391.

31 It is common in nomadic cultures worldwide for women to be responsible for the creation and upkeep of the soft parts of shelter. In Central Asia, women are in charge of the felting process, which is a community event. They also patch the felt when it wears thin and completely replace it every five years. In Turkic tribes, women weave the belts that hold the yurt together and the rugs that go inside.

32 In Chingiz Khan's day, visiting dignitaries were given repeated warnings not to step on the threshold, and anyone who stepped on the threshold of a leader's ger was put to death. Andrews, FT&P, 475.

33 "Throughout Siberian as well as among many Native American groups people believe that there are three worlds laid upon one another in the universe. In some ways, ideas about the upper and lower worlds seem to imply a concept of parallel worlds rather than that of three worlds being literally stacked like layers on a cake.... In some shaman rituals, such as the initiation of shamans in Buryatia, a tree will actually be erected extending from beside the gal golomt [central fire] to beyond the smokehole." See the "Course in Mongolian Shamanism" Web site: http://members.tripod.com/Mongolian_page/shaman.txt.

34 "The universe of the Mongols can be visualized as a circle, not only in the three dimensions, but also in time itself. Everything has a circular motion, the path of the sun from day to day, the cycle of time from year to year, and the cycle of all living spirits as they return to the earth to live again and again. Intersecting the circle are the axes of the four directions and the axis of the center of the world going up to the upper world beyond the eternal heavens and going down beyond Mother Earth to the lower world." Ibid.

35 There are "repeated references to the door of a trellis tent turned to the sunrise...recalling early Mongol practice." Andrews, FT&P 480. "As suggested by the 'Secret History,' the transition from the eastward orientation...to the southward one was evidently complete by the thirteenth century, under Chinese influence." Andrews, FT&P, 474.

36 Willem van Rubruck, on second French mission of 1253–55 to Mongolia. Andrews, FT&P, 484. These associations are also reflected in Native American traditions.

37 *Tegsh* in Khalkha Mongolian means "level, equal, tranquil, a sense of order." Quoted from notes provided by Peter Alford Andrews to author. "Mongols believe that the goal of life is to live tegsh, in balance with the world. One stands alone and in power at the center of the world, with infinite blue Father heaven above and Mother Earth supporting and nurturing below. By living an upright and respectful life, human beings will keep their world in balance and maximize their personal power." See the "Course in Mongolian Shamanism" Web site.

chapter 3: the tapered wall yurt

* See, for example, Gyorgy Doczi, *The Power of Limits: Proportional Harmonies in Nature, Art, and Architecture* (Boston: Shambhala, 2005) and Christopher Alexander, *The Nature of Order, Book 1: The Phenomena of Life* (Berkeley: Center for Environmental Structure, 2002).

chapter 4: the modern fabric yurt

1 Tree-planter and mathematician Charlie Crawford produced an eighty-seven-page set of yurt plans in 1978 that he called *The Yurt and I.* Crawford also built many Hoedad yurts.

2 Lodgepole pine has a couple of advantages: the whole log is used, making the rafter stronger than dimensional lumber because the grain of the wood is never cut. It's also environmentally friendly; lodgepole (or "jack") pine functions as a nurse tree in new forest growth and must be thinned to allow room for other species.

3 These Web sites have helpful information on electric bear fencing: www.sureguard.com.au/electric_fence_design.html and www.nols.edu/resources/research.

4 Pacific Yurts and Yurtco have designs for a moveable deck. To see step-by-step photos of a portable platform being built, see *Lars' Yurt Page* at www.rdrop.com/~glacier/yurt.htm.

5 Colorado Yurt Company has developed a system for opening their zippered flaps from ground level.

6 Most of the yurt companies supply plans for an SIP platform. Yurtco sells an SIP platform made in sections and connected with splines, making it very portable. Colorado Yurt Company also sells complete SIP decks.

7 It may seem simpler to build a large deck and then build the smaller circular platform for the yurt on top of the deck. However, this uses extra materials, costs more, and may require additional building time. Most of the yurt companies do not recommend this option, except when building a wood-frame radiant-heat floor. Yurtco suggests building a large deck first in conjunction with their portable floor.

8 For a helpful summary of holistic site considerations, see Dan Chiras' book, *The Natural House*, Chapter 15, "Site Considerations," 385–419. The book also contains helpful sections on everything from solar orientation to alternative energy, water, and waste systems. Christopher Alexander, in *A Pattern Language*, proposes siting a home on the part of your land that needs the most attention and healing (i.e., the weakest area rather than the strongest, which we normally seek out for siting).

9 To keep down creosote, try burning creosote-destroying fire logs or granules, which you can pick up at a hardware or farm store.

10 Before purchasing a propane heater, make sure that the BTU rating is sufficient for the size of your space.

11 If you want to "try before you buy," Canadian manufacturer Yurtco has a sister company, Canadian Yurts, that provides long-term rentals to campsites and parks. See the Resource Guide under "Yurt Companies" for company information.

12 Other possibilities for the third and final layer include the brands ThermaBond, ThermTech, and Thermax.

13 British yurt-maker and designer Hal Wynne-Jones has this to say about yurt companies: "The accessibility of yurts to everyone—no patents, no copyright, no big investment—also brings its problems. Not all yurt makers fully understand or are willing and able to discharge the responsibilities that go with being the builder of someone's home. There is a difference between making your own yurt and selling one. The prices that the established builders charge reflect their expertise, investment, and follow-up service. Newcomers to yurt building can be enticed by the seemingly high prices [charged for yurts], yet fail to deliver the necessary quality of service. There is no solution to this as of yet other than caveat emptor."

14 See the Resource Guide for information on composting toilets. For information on the sawdust toilet, see *The Humanure Handbook: A Guide to Composting Human Manure* by Joseph © Jenkins. This excellent book explains everything you need to know to use this method safely and successfully.

15 Most US building officials use either the UBC (Uniform Building Code) or one of the new ICC (International Code Council) rulebooks. The two ICC rulebooks are the residential IRC (International Residential Code) and the commercial IBC (International Building Code). The IRC and IBC were updated in 2003 and again in 2006. Some states require use of the most current code, although this takes a year or two to implement. Most of the insulation requirements are contained in an additional code book called the *International Energy Conservation Code*. For excerpts from the code books, see Appendix 1.

16 Less than 25 percent of a building's heat loss or gain is conductive. Mass-type insulation is up to 95 percent effective for reducing conductive heat loss. Over 75 percent of heat loss or gain is radiant. Reflective insulation reduces reflective heat loss by as much as 97 percent; mass-type insulation reduces it by only by 5 to 10 percent. One test showed reflective insulation to be more than seven times as effective as R-19 conductive insulation. (Information flyer "Foil Insulation," Yurtco Manufacturing, Inc.)

17 If you have a "100-percent heating appliance" (e.g., a propane heater that keeps the yurt at a constant 70 degrees and therefore keeps the snow melted off the roof), you may be able to get away with much lower insulation requirements.

18 Energy codes were developed primarily to conserve natural resources (particularly nonrenewable resources). Pellet stoves are an example of a heating method that utilizes a renewable resource: the pellets are made from an agricultural product that used to be "waste." Other examples are woodstoves using dead or thinned trees and electric heaters run with power generated by wind or water. People have been exempted from insulation requirements when generating their own power to run heaters.

SELECTED BIBLIOGRAPHY

Following are selected works that are not included in the Resource Guide but that are part of the body of research.

BOOKS

Alexander, Christopher. *A Pattern Language*. London: Oxford University Press, 1977.

——. *The Phenomenon of Life*. The Nature of Order Series, Book 1. Berkeley: Center for Environmental Structure, 2003.

Bartholomew, Therese T., ed. *Mongolia: The Legacy of Chinggis Khan*. San Francisco: Thames and Hudson, Asian Art Museum of San Francisco, 1995.

Becker, Jasper. *The Lost Country*. New York: Scepter, 1993. London: Hodder & Stoughton, 1995.

Bidder, Irmgard, and Hans Bidder. *Filzteppiche: Ihre Geschichte und Eigenart*. Germany: Klinkhardt & Biermann, 1980.

Bowden, C. R. *The Modern History of Mongolia*. London: Praeger Publishing, 1968. Reprint 1989.

Breeden, Robert L. *Nomads of the World*. Washington: National Geographic Society, 1971.

Brill, Marlene Targe. *Mongolia*. Danbury, CT: Children's Press, 1992.

Burkett, M. E. *The Art of the Feltmaker*. Kenda, Cumbria, England: Abbot Halt Art Gallery, 1979.

Cammann, Schuyler. *The Land of the Camel: Tents and Temples of Inner Mongolia*. NY: Ronald Press, 1951.

Doczi, Gyorgy. *The Power of Limits: Proportional Harmonies*. Boston: Shambhala Publications, 1981.

Drinkard, G. Lawson III. *Retreats: Handmade Hideaways to Refresh the Spirit*. Salt Lake City, UT: Gibbs Smith, Publisher, 1997.

Ekvall, Robert B. *Fields on the Hoof: Nexus of Tibetan Nomadic Pastoralism*. NY: Holt, Rinehart and Winston, 1968.

Gold, Peter. *Navaho and Tibetan Sacred Wisdom: The Circle of the Spirit*. Rochester, VT: Inner Traditions, 1994.

Goldstein, Melvyn C., and Cynthia M. Beall. *Nomads of Western Tibet: The Survival of a Way of Life*. Berkeley: University of California Press, 1990.

Haslund, Henning. *In Secret Mongolia*. London: Kegan Paul, 1934. Reprint: Adventures Unlimited Press, 1995.

Jones, Shirley Ann, ed. *Simply Living: The Spirit of the Indigenous People*. Novato, CA: New World Library, 1999.

Keenan, George. *Tent Life in Siberia: A New Account of an Old Undertaking*. Russia Observed, Series 1. Philadelphia: Ayer Press, 1872. Reprint 1911, 1970.

Nabakov, Peter, and Robert Easton. *Native American Architecture*. NY/Oxford: Oxford University Press, 1989.

Olcott, Martha B. *The Kazakhs*. 2nd ed. Stanford, CA: Hoover Institute Press, 1995.

Oliver, Paul, ed. *Encyclopedia of Vernacular Architecture of the World*. Vol. 1–3: Cambridge University Press, 1998.

Schneider, Michael S. *A Beginner's Guide to Constructing the Universe: The Mathematical Archetypes of Nature, Art and Science*. New York: Harper Paperbacks, 1995.

Sjoberg, Gunilla Paetau. *New Directions for Felt: An Ancient Craft*. Translated by Patricia Spark. Loveland, CO: Interweave Press, 1996.

Thybony, Scott. *The Hogan: The Traditional Navajo Home*. Tucson: Western National Parks Association, 1999.

Vreelan, Herbert H. III. *Mongol Community and Kinship Structure*. Newhaven, CT: HRAF Press, 1962.

ARTICLES

The following articles come from *National Geographic*.

January 1936. Murray, Edward. "With the Nomads of Central Asia." Vol. 69, no. 1, 1–57.

March 1962. Douglas, William O. "Journey to Outer Mongolia." Vol. 121, no. 3, 289–345.

April 1972. Michaud, Sabrina, and Roland Michaud. "Winter Caravan to the 'Roof of the World." 435–65.

Spring 1973. Hallet, Stanley I., and Rafi Samizay. "Context of Man: The Yurt of Afghanistan," University of Utah Department of Architecture: Utah Chapter of AIA.

May 1988. Hyde, Nina. "Wool: Fabric of History." Vol. 173, no.5, 552–91.

May 1993. Beall, Cynthia, and Melvyn Goldstein. "Mongolian Nomads." Vol. 183, no. 5, 127–36.

December 1996. Edwards, Mike. "Genghis Khan: Lord of the Mongols." Vol. 190, no. 6, 2–35.

February 1997. "Genghis Kahn," part II.

March 1998. Montaigne, Fen. "Nomads of the Arctic." Vol. 193, no. 3, 120–37.

July 1999. Montaigne, Fen. "Iran: Testing the Waters of Reform." Vol. 196, no. 1, 2–33.

September 1999. Millard, Candace S. "Mongolian Eagle Hunters." Vol. 196, no. 3, 90–103.

May 2001. Edwards, Mike. "Marco Polo: Venice to China." Vol. 199, no. 5, 2–31.

June 2001. Edwards, Mike. "Marco Polo II: In China." Vol. 199, no. 6, 20–45.

PHOTO CREDITS

Front Cover: © Colorado Yurt Company, www.coloradoyurt.com

Back Cover: © Scott Vlaun, www.moosepond-arts.com, yurt by Oregon Yurtworks, www.yurtworks.com

p. ix: Peter Forbes, www.wholecommunities.org

p. xiii: © Colorado Yurt Company, www.coloradoyurt.com

p. xiv: © Jeff Suhy, www.robotandsons.com

p. 2: top photo © Karie Knoke; bottom photo © Bill Coperthwaite Collection

p. 3: diagram top left © Aaron Qualls; photo bottom right © Christine Seashore and Jon Turk, www.jonturk.net

p. 4: photo bottom left © P. A. Andrews, http://peterandrews.info; photo bottom right © Dan Neumeyer, JADE Craftsman Builders, www.jadedesignbuild.com

p. 6: photo top left © Bill Coperthwaite collection; photo bottom right © Canyonlands Field Institute, Professor Valley Field Camp, www.canyonlandsfieldinst.org

p. 7: photo top right © Scott Vlaun; photo bottom right © Bill Lubarsky

p. 8: photos top right © Hal Wynne-Jones collection, Turkoman Yurts, www.turkomangers.co.uk; diagram middle right © Hal Wynne-Jones; photo bottom left © the Scottish Storytelling Yurt, www.scottishstorytellingyurt.co.uk

p. 9: top right photo sequence: photo top left © Charles Leys, Atelier Trois Yourtes, www.yourtes.fr; photo top right © Rob Matthews, the Yurt Workshop, www.yurtworkshop.com; photo middle right © Yurtworks, www.yurtworks.co.uk; photo bottom © Steve Place, Handmade Hardwood Yurts, www.fsnet.co.uk; photo middle left © Charles Leys; bottom left photo sequence: photo far left © Charles Leys; photo top right © Rob Matthews; photo middle right © Paul King, Woodland Yurts, www.woodlandyurts.co.uk; photo bottom right © Alexandr Spado, Workshop Under the Hill, www.yourtent.com

p. 10, 11: photos © Scott Vlaun, yurt by California Yurts, www.yurtpeople.com

p. 12: photo © Scott Vlaun, yurt by Oregon Yurtworks, www.yurtworks.com

p. 13: diagram courtesy of Pacific Yurts, Inc., Cottage Grove, Oregon, www.yurts.com

p. 14: photo collage: photo top left © Dan Neumeyer; photo top right © Paul King; photo bottom right © Dan Neumeyer; photo bottom left © Beth and Larry Beede

p. 16: photo © Dan Neumeyer

p. 18: all photos © Dan Neumeyer

p. 19: diagram © Torvald Faegre

p. 21: painting of Nogay cart tents, vans, and trellis tents in the Volga Steppe, 1793–94, by © G. H. Geissler, from P. S. Pallas 1799–1801, photo © P. A. Andrews

p. 22: diagram top left © Torvald Faegre; photo sequence middle right © Paul King; photo bottom right © Paul King

p. 23: photos top left, top right, and bottom right © P. A. Andrews; photo bottom left © Joanne Warfield, "The Beauty of Afghanistan Remembered" portfolio, 1977, www.JoanneWarfieldFineArt.com

p. 24: thumbnail sequence photos © Paul King; photo middle right © P. A. Andrews

p. 25: photo © Dan Neumeyer

p. 26: photo top right © P. A. Andrews; bottom photo © Dan Neumeyer

p. 27: photo © Dan Neumeyer

p. 28: painting © Chris McKee, www.mujaan.com

p. 29: photo lower left © Dan Neumeyer; photo sequence lower right © Paul King

p. 30: photos top left and top right © P. A. Andrews; bottom photo © Christine Seashore and Jon Turk

p. 31–32: photos © Beth and Larry Beede

p. 33: felting photo sequence © Paul King; photo lower right © Beth and Larry Beede

p. 34–35: photo © Chris Mckee

p. 36: top three photos © P. A. Andrews; bottom photo © Dan Neumeyer

p. 37: diagram © Torvald Faegre

p. 38: wooden image © collection of Irkutsk Museum of Wooden Architecture, Taltsi

p. 40: photo © Bill Coperthwaite collection

p. 42: photo top left © Peter Forbes, www.wholecommunities.org; photo bottom left © Dan Neumeyer

p. 43: photo top right © Robin Li; photo bottom right © Peter Forbes; photo bottom left © Robin Li

p. 44: photo top right © Bill Coperthwaite collection; photo lower right © becky kemery

p. 45: photo upper and lower right © Peter Forbes; photo lower left © Bill Coperthwaite collection

p. 46: photo © Bill Coperthwaite collection, Abbie Sewall, photographer

p. 47: all photos © Bill Coperthwaite collection; photo top right Jim Ceteras, photographer; photo top right Merle Bruno, photographer

p. 48: yurt plans and drawings © Bill Coperthwaite, drawings by Torvald Faegre

p. 49, 51: photos © Julie Pratt

p. 52: Jewel Yurt sketch and blueprints © Dan Neumeyer, JADE Craftsman Builders, www.jadedesignbuild.com

p. 54: photos © Bill Coperthwaite collection; photo bottom left Dorothy Cox, photographer

p. 55: photos © Bill Coperthwaite collection; photo bottom right Aaiyn Foster, photographer

p. 56: photos © Bill Coperthwaite collection; photo bottom right Jim Underwood, photographer

p. 57: photos © Bill Coperthwaite collection; top photo Jim Underwood, photographer

p. 58: thumbnail sequence © Future Generations India, www.future.org; bottom photo © Dave Kirkpatrick

p. 59, 60, 61, 63: yurt designed by John Nance family, tricentricyurt@google.com, photos © Scott Vlaun

p. 62: Tricentric Yurt blueprints © John Nance

p. 64: top photo © Yurtco Mfg., Inc., www.yurtco.com; bottom photo © Falling Waters Resort

p. 66: photo © Colorado Yurt Company

p. 67: Exploded View Diagram courtesy of Pacific Yurts, Inc.

p. 68: photo © becky kemery

p. 69: photo © Jerry Gray, Red Mountain Lodge Works, Lake City, CO

p. 70: photo © Kris Ernest and Dan Beck

p. 71: photo © Douglas Nelson

p. 72: photo top left © Debra Amerson, www.plantris.com.; photo top right © Scott Vlaun, yurt from www.oceansong.org; photo bottom right © Sacred Groves Eco-Retreat Center, www.sacredgroves.com, and © Linda Wolf, photographer, www.lindawolf.net

p. 73: photo © Karie Knoke

p. 74: middle left © Canyonlands Field Institute, Professor Valley Field Camp, www.canyonlandsfieldinst.org; bottom right © Ed Kornbrath, www.edkdesign.com

p. 75: photo top right © Falling Waters Resort, www.fallingwatersresort.com; photo bottom right © Cedar House Inn and Yurts, www.georgiamountaininn.com

p. 76: photo © Falling Waters Resort

p. 77: photo © Viking Yurt Restaurant, www.vikingyurt.com

p. 78: photo © Colorado Yurt Company, www.coloradoyurt.com

p. 82: photo middle left © Pacific Yurts, Inc.; photo top right © Oregon Parks and Recreation Department, www.oregonstateparks.org; floor plan lower right © Pacific Yurts, Inc.

p. 83: photographed by Cliff and Jean Dickey, © Florrisant Fossil Beds National Monument, www.nps.gov/flfo

p. 84: photo © Colorado Yurt Company

p. 88: photo top right © Colorado Yurt Company; photo bottom left © Colorado Yurt Company

p. 89: photos © Bill Lubarsky

p. 91: photo © Colorado Yurt Company

p. 92: photos © Joseph Boud

p. 94: photo © Cheryl Haines, For/site Foundation, www.for-site.org

p. 97: photo sequence © Mt. Orford Ski Resort, Quebec, www.orford.com.; lower right photo © Rainier Yurts, www.rainier.com

p. 99: photo © Nomad Shelter Yurts, www.nomadshelter.com

p. 100, 102, 103, 104, 105, 106, 107, 109, 112, 113, 114, 115, 116: photos © Scott Vlaun, www.moosepondarts.com

p. 110, 111: floor plans © Oregon Yurtworks, www.yurtworks.com

p. 118: photo © Yurtworks, www.yurtworks.co.uk

p. 119: photos © Yurtco Mfg., Inc.

p. 120: top photo © Rainier Yurts; bottom left floor plan © Pacific Yurts, Inc.; bottom right photo © Scott Vlaun, La Casita Ridgetop Retreat Yurt at Terri's Homestay Bed and Breakfast, Point Reyes National Park, CA, www.terrishomestay.com

p. 121: photo top left © Yurtworks; photo bottom right © Colorado Yurt Company

p. 122: photo © Elisabeth Wasserman

Appendix 2: diagrams and information courtesy of Pacific Yurts, Inc.

Appendix 3: diagram and information courtesy of Pacific Yurts, Inc.

144